Prais

Genius Spark provides a beacon of insight in a world hungry for transformation. It's not just a concept; it's a catalyst that's taken my aspirations to new heights. The Genius Paragraph is my daily roadmap, shaping how I navigate the world. With Rex's guidance and the Spark's innovation, I've harnessed personal development like never before—knowledge into action, potential into reality, all through the art of reflection. A few minutes daily, a lifetime of impact.

—Bill Seed, SVP Facilities Design & Construction at Jackson Health System

For over 20 years I have been an admirer of Rex Miller. There are very few people who are as curious and as capable at making connections as Rex. Whether it is making a connection between the neglected but inherent capacities of human beings or helping you connect to what makes you "spark", Rex's insights fill this book—and will fill your own life—with hope, energy, and possibility.

—Tod Bolsinger, Co-Founder of AE Sloan Leadership, author of *Tempered Resilience: How Leaders are Formed in the Crucible of Change*.

I've been captivated by Rex's evolution as a coach over the past two decades. In various contexts, I've witnessed him enter a room armed with little more than StrengthsFinder results, seemingly conjuring magic as he precisely identifies ways to significantly enhance team performance. Having gained insight into his methods, I've come to recognize that his achievements stem largely from his unique toolkit and strategies. This book provides us with direct entry into Rex's toolkit, empowering us to become more effective leaders.

—Craig Janssen, Principal at Salas O'Brien

Over the last decade, Rex's work with me, and his innovation with Genius Spark transformed my understanding of unlocking potential and the role of leadership. It guided me in cultivating my own talents into strengths and showed me the profound importance of empowering others. This book is a roadmap for unlocking hidden potential and growth in oneself and those we lead. Rex's book and system ignite the spark of personal and collective excellence.

—Mark Konchar, President, US Civils & Managing Director of US Rail at Balfour Beatty

Fifteen years ago, Rex introduced a strengths-based approach to examine the leadership team which we were able to use to enhance our insights in how to best leverage each other's talents. Recently, I asked Rex to take our leadership team through his newly developed Genius Spark. The process was simple and offered insights to our individual and collective team leadership dynamics. Because the process was simplified, Genius Spark was a more economical approach without sacrifice of the useful insights.

—Eric Stenman, President and Chief Executive Officer, Balfour Beatty US

Beyond mere motivation, The Genius Spark unveils a roadmap to enlightenment, guiding us to transcend perceived boundaries. Through harnessing our inherent strengths and fostering a mindset of growth, we shatter limitations. Miller has masterfully created an indispensable guide for leaders aspiring to embolden their teams, navigate change, and attain enduring greatness. Move beyond passing trends – uncover the timeless key to profound transformation within The Genius Spark."

Joseph R. Myers, Best-selling author of Trust and The Search to Belong

I've seen firsthand how Rex Miller's Genius Spark process changes people's internal dialogue and the dynamics on a team - it's like a burst of oxygen and generates forward momentum where things seem intractable.

—Michelle Kinder, M.Ed., LPC, ACC - CEO of Embody EQ

The Genius Spark is just exactly that... A book to ignite the genius inside you. Rex gives a mix of fun stories with insightful facts to give encouragement and practical tips to use your strength, discover your self, and ultimately live on purpose with purpose.

—Emily Elrod, CEO of Workzbe

As an Executive Coach and Leadership Consultant, I've found the Genius Spark to be the bedrock upon which I elevate leaders and their teams. In the realm of leadership, fostering self-awareness is paramount, a cornerstone of trust-building. This is precisely where the Genius Spark shines. It's a versatile instrument that not only sets the stage for individual, team, and project transformation, but also cultivates a culture of growth. If you and your team are committed to ascension, the Genius Spark is the definitive choice.

—Stan Gibson, Founder of OxygenPlus Consulting

I've been a strong advocate for strengths assessments as a tool for making sense of ourselves and the world around us. The Genius Spark framework takes this to the next level by making assessment outcomes accessible and personalized. This makes them even more powerful and meaningful to users and increases the likelihood that they'll be taken to heart, improving relationships and driving better results. GeniusSpark is a great tool for anyone looking to become better!"

**—Markku Allison, Vice President,
Strategy + Innovation at Chandos Construction**

Unlocking your potential requires plumbing the depths within, an insight that charts your course to fulfillment. This only becomes evident when you fully understand and accept what makes you unique and valuable. But how do you get there? Genius Spark is your guide on this journey of self-discovery and potential and, more importantly, provides the key to unlocking what is already in you.

—Mike Muhney, Co-inventor of ACT! software, creator of the CRM industry.

Rex Miller's Genius Spark is a captivating journey told through relatable stories, embedding a reliable methodology into everyday life. His FAA success story is both humorous and insightful. The process is simple, sustainable, and essential for anyone seeking to rediscover their genius.

—Gary Corbett, Founder and Chief Strategist for Group C Advisors

When it comes to leading and inspiring people, there is no shortage of self-proclaimed experts and books on the subject. Personally, I've come across many of them in my time. Out of that long list, Genius Spark alone focuses on unlocking potential and empowering individuals to become the heroes of their own futures, while also cultivating teams of heroes.

This refreshing perspective stands in stark contrast to the experts and self-proclaimed heroes who centered the conversation around themselves. It's a departure from the tired rhetoric of "I don't know how to do your job, but my book says you're doing it wrong!"

—Bill Black, President and COO of the Calgary Construction Association

Rex's inspiring book guides readers to unlock their inner genius and live up to their full potential. Through relatable stories and practical insights, Rex provides a roadmap to self-discovery that will resonate with anyone seeking purpose and meaning. Read this book to reignite your creativity, innovation, and limitless possibility.

—Chaz Horn, Founder - Mastery Of B2B Sales

Rex has released a revolutionary method for uncovering your life's spark, your very genius. Within these pages of inspiration, he steers you toward recognizing, honing, and amplifying your distinctive strengths and talents, leading you to a life of meaning and accomplishment.

—Mike Coleman, Cofounder and former CEO of Integrity Media

genius SPARK

Meteor Education LLC 690 NE 23rd Ave, Gainesville, FL 32609
meteoreducationpublishing.com

Meteor Education Publishing is a division or Meteor Education. The name and logo are trademarks of Meteor Education.

Cover and internal design: Mayfly Design

Illustrations: Michael Lagocki - www.michaellagocki.com

ISBN Paperback - 978-1-7334334-3-3
eBook - 979-8-9894567-0-3

Library of Congress Control Number: 2023921119

Printed in the United States of America

genius
SPARK

REIGNITE YOUR LIFE

rex MILLER

METEOR EDUCATION

To Mrs. Stavoe,
Who first noticed the storyteller within me and nurtured my curiosity as a child, seeing possibilities I had not yet imagined.

To Mr. Roubidoux,
Who ignited in me a spirit of excellence and showed me I had too much potential to let it go to waste.

And to Michael Vance,
Whose wisdom taught me to embrace my originality and uniqueness. He was the first to give language and insight to the genius spark waiting to be unleashed.

This book stands upon your shoulders. Your belief in my untapped brilliance lit the first sparks that years later have grown into a creative blaze. You saw the genius within me even when I could not yet see it myself.

May this work pass on the gifts you first gave me—to notice unseen potential, awaken dreams, and empower others to boldly shine their inner light.

With gratitude,
Rex

Foreword

When I began working closely with Rex Miller almost a decade ago, little did I realize the profound impact that tapping into individuals' inner genius could have on our entire organization. In almost every conversation with different teams in our organization today, a common thread emerges: people deeply value being acknowledged and appreciated by their leaders and peers for their unique contributions and talents. When individuals are free to embrace their strengths, their best work often seems like a magic trick to those around them. It's akin to pulling rabbits out of hats, leaving us all in awe. But this isn't magic; it's the embodiment of their inner genius—the purest expression of their innate talents.

During these pandemic years, our organization has been eager to take these concepts even further as the realities of remote work and prolonged recovery have created new challenges. Recognizing that lasting change requires a process, not just better information, I was thrilled to engage the strategies and tools of the Genius Spark. Building on Rex's work with thousands of individuals across diverse organizations like ours, Genius Spark introduces a guided process that unlocks untapped potential through consistent practice and reflection on one's journey toward peak performance. By helping individuals create their own "Genius portrait" and engaging with it regularly, remarkable progress becomes a daily reality for our teams.

The Genius Process helps leaders fit all their pieces together by uniting a team around shared strengths and individual contributions. For our journey it has nurtured a common language across our organization and fostered a vibrant and unified culture at our core. The transformation sparked by Genius Spark is clear—seen not only in playful strengths-based nicknames and symbols but also in concrete achievements. This results in increased engagement, strong collaboration, and remarkable accomplishments that drive our growth while preserving our authenticity and purpose.

However, we don't just envision the impact of Genius Spark in our workplace; our vision extends into the realm of education. The erosion of creative confidence often creeps into formal education, leaving a mere fraction of those who come through the other side possessing the audacity of their bold and creative childlike selves. This is why our commitment remains steadfast in introducing the Genius Spark program to students—offering them the chance to nurture their budding talents and preserve their innate brilliance.

Genius Spark stands as a testament to the extraordinary potential that resides within each of us. It's a guide that rekindles the spark of brilliance, no matter where you stand in life's journey. The earlier you embark on this path, the more time you have to amplify your unique talents. Rex's insights into scaling strengths-based learning are revolutionary, reshaping organizational dynamics and redefining educational paradigms.

I encourage you to embrace this transformative voyage—a journey to rediscover the latent magic within you. Moreover, I would encourage leaders to imagine the possibility of your team tapping into their best potential. Witness the revival of the spark that illuminated your childhood, and harness your talents to shape a life of exceptional impact and purpose. Good luck with your own Genius journey!

With unwavering conviction,
Bill Latham
Founder and CEO, Meteor Education

Contents

Preface

The Spark Within

What if I told you that buried inside each of us is a creative genius just waiting to be unleashed? As children, we all exhibited the unbridled imagination, curiosity, and confidence that characterize the minds of young prodigies. But a strange thing happens as we grow up. The boundless creativity of our youth somehow fades beneath layers of societal conditioning, routine, and self-doubt. We learn to fit in rather than stand out. Our inner spark dims.

But what if it didn't have to be this way? What if we could reclaim that childhood genius even in adulthood?

This book serves as a guide along that profound path of self-discovery. By examining the lives of pioneering figures who never lost their creative fire, this work aims to reignite your passion and potential. The pages ahead provide insights and tools to rewire thought patterns, realign with your core purpose, and unlock the extraordinary power within you. Your untold story waits inside—now is the time to write it. May this book spark the flames of creativity and empowerment, lighting your path to lifelong fulfillment. The journey begins here.

Introduction

Welcome to the Genius Spark

We don't grow into creativity, we grow out of it. Or rather, we get educated out of it.

—Sir Ken Robinson

Looking Back: Rachel's Story

Rachel walks through her parents' living room in the house where she grew up, passing the wall of portraits her mother lovingly arranged into a family Hall of Fame. First up is a kindergarten class picture. Her hair was bright blonde at that age, so she's easy to spot in the front row, arms wrapped around her best friend in a neck-crunching hug. She always connected quickly with others. The next photo is her first softball game, seven years old and face set in firm determination, her green eyes locked onto the oncoming ball. It's easy to see she was one confident, motivated kid.

In another frame is a gangly thirteen-year-old, almost ready to enter high school. This young lady is a bit harder to read, but you can still tell from the way she's standing, one hand on the red strap of her backpack, looking over her left shoulder as she climbs the steps to the school bus, that Rachel is someone who can make sense of the world. She naturally sees things in terms of patterns and categories, and she is clearly goal-oriented and driven. Her eyes survey the scene, assess the situation, and decide how to proceed. Looking at this picture, you get the sense that high school is going to go just fine for Rachel.

She's passed by these pictures a thousand times before, and yet, looking at them now gives her a lump in her throat. The room is quiet and dim in the evening light, but Rachel's inner voice is anything but calm.

"What the hell happened to me?" she wonders.

"I was such a charming little genius! Well, maybe not a true GENIUS in the dictionary definition, but still. I was bright, creative, funny, and SO helpful to other students and my friends. I looked at the world with wonder and hope and opportunity. No matter what I tried, I knew I didn't have to be perfect at it right away. If I cared about it, that was enough. I was always in motion, always moving forward, and I didn't need success all at once."

As the questions flow through Rachel's mind, she is already answering herself.

"I mean, it's not all bad, is it?" she wonders. "I worked hard in high school, got good grades, and went to a good college. Sure, I wasn't SUPER excited about quitting softball to take more honors classes, but they paid off. I didn't love those AP Calculus study sessions, but I aced the national exam and got college credit. And now look at me! I work at a well-known accounting firm, and I'm good at my job. We have a nice house in a great neighborhood. We've raised two wonderful kids, as well as that silly but adorable dog. We take vacations. We're never hungry. Life is good. So, why am I staring at these pictures, pining for my childhood?"

Rachel sighs.

It's not that she's MISERABLE—she's just feeling a bit lost. Everything takes so much effort. Days seem to blend together. Life is a constant blur of to-do lists and spreadsheets, meetings and more meetings. If she just stopped doing it all, would it even matter? Would anyone notice?

The pictures remind her of something, a time when what she wanted just seemed easy and attainable. She has a sneaking suspicion that if she could just tap into some of what she used to have, used to be, things would be better. Although she's seen the wall a thousand times before, this time she's drawn toward her seven-year-old self, that crooked grin, those innocent eyes. Then she hears her inner voice again: "Hey, kid; what the hell happened to you?"

If she knew what happened, she'd be able to answer all these *questions* that keep popping into her head:

Where did that joy go?
What am I actually good at?
What truly energizes and excites me?
What happened to my younger self?
How can I get her back?

Rachel isn't sure, but she won't find the answers while staring at that wall. She leaves the living room and heads for the kitchen and dinner with her parents, a monthly routine. They talk about the usual things. Work is fine. The kids are great. Yeah, maybe Florida this year. The pictures hang in the slowly darkening room, the fading sunlight a fading reminder of a girl who became a woman, and in the process lost contact with the things that made her a genius.

Unleashing Our Uniqueness: A Lesson from Walt Disney

Rachel's story isn't unusual or unique. Vast numbers of adults the world over experience moments of dissatisfaction, a lack of certainty about their personal and professional direction, and, above all else, a sneaking suspicion that something is missing, that there is MORE out there. It may sound cliché, but we all have the necessary potential to find whatever the 'MORE' is that we're looking for. We all have a spark, a "Genius Spark," a little fire that's been with us since we were children. If we could just see it, there'd be no darkness we couldn't light up.

Mike Vance, a former dean of Disney University, once asked Walt Disney, "How does a person stay creative?" Disney's answer: "The more you are like yourself, the less you are like anyone else, which makes you unique." Of the billions of people who have ever lived, there is no one quite like each one of us. And, if there is one thing we should all be good at, it's being us, being our own unique selves. Later, Uncle Walt told Vance, "The problem with most people is they spend their lives trying to emulate others, so we have lots of copies but few originals." Vance carried that lesson throughout the rest of his life, always remembering to focus on his originality and helping people find it in themselves. When I met Mike in the early 1980s, he told me something I've never forgotten: "It is the uniqueness factor that people are attracted to. Nobody wants to go to *kind-of-like* Disney."

Vance embodied the spirit of genius and exuded an infectious zest for life. I had never met anyone so naturally curious and creative. He was attracted to and became intimately familiar with many well-known geniuses from his boss Walt Disney to renowned architect, inventor, writer, and philosopher Buckminster Fuller. Mike spent a lot of time studying geniuses from throughout history—people like innovative educator Maria Montessori and the artist and inventor Leonardo da Vinci. Well before Google developed its research program, Project Aristotle, to help understand why some people succeed while others struggle, Mike Vance understood everyone contains a Genius Spark that emerges naturally under the right conditions and in the right environment. That insight, passed from Walt Disney to Mike Vance, and then from Mike to me, ignited the inspiration for *The Genius Spark*. In fact, it was the spark that lit this flame.

The Dilemma: Fitting In or Standing Out

From birth, we are rewarded for behaving and performing within a range of norms: crawling, walking, speaking, reading, and socializing are the metrics others use to measure our progress. By the time we enter school, those metrics have turned into grades, activities, interests, and relationships, specifically the kind of friends we made. Those measurements, which are designed to help us fit in, also begin to limit and narrow the unique qualities that make us who we are. And the deeper we go into school, the more likely we are to conform to what is expected of us to be instead of focusing on developing the gifts, the "genius," we already have.

In the 1960s, author and general systems scientist George Land began studying creative performance qualities in people. He developed the Imaginative Index, a creativity test that NASA used to identify particularly innovative scientists and engineers. In 1968, out of general scientific curiosity, Land administered that NASA creativity assessment to a group of 1,600 Pre-K students, intending to study the creativity of young children. When preschoolers took the assessment, "98 percent scored at 'creative genius' level."[1] The same test assessment was administered again once the children were a little older. "Five years later, only 30 percent of the same group of children scored at the same level, and again, five years later, only 12 percent. When the same test was administered to adults, it was found that only two percent scored at this genius level. According to the study, our creativity is drained by our education." Land's results provide evidence that creativity is inherently human, and that rather than focusing on *teaching* creativity, we should focus on *unlearning* non-creative habits and mindsets. I would suggest that many of the tendencies children exhibit around creativity are the same tendencies that, if projected forward, would allow adults to more frequently, and more intentionally, tap into their Genius Spark.

Sir Ken Robinson, an esteemed British author and education reformer, believed what Land's study had suggested. He researched, understood, and advocated for the power and importance of children's natural, genius-level creativity. In 2007 Robinson delivered the most viewed TED Talk in history—"Do Schools Kill Creativity?" In his talk, Robinson masterfully references Land's study and delves into whether the education system is partially responsible for the documented loss of genius. As individuals, we may not be entirely sure of why or when it happened, but if we take a moment to reflect on whether we have the same level of enthusiasm,

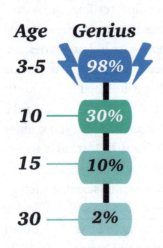

Age	Genius
3-5	98%
10	30%
15	10%
30	2%

1. Rohini Venkatraman, "You're 96 Percent Less Creative Than You Were as a Child. Here's How to Reverse That," *Inc.com*, January 18, 2018, https://www.inc.com/rohini-venkatraman/4-ways-to-get-back-creativity-you-had-as-a-kid.html.

curiosity, and joy for life that we had as young children, the answer is most often a resounding "No."

The wonder and magic of childhood have been extensively studied and documented. In childhood we are particularly receptive to new information and experiences, and we quickly incorporate them into our understanding of the world and our place within it. In fact, if you ask a group of kindergartners whether they want to draw or sing or dance or play pretend, they will enthusiastically agree. Genius artist Pablo Picasso knew this well. When talking about art and creativity Picasso once said, "Every child is an artist. The problem is how to remain an artist once we grow up." The developmental period of early childhood is vital for our long-term physical, emotional, and mental well-being. It is also, as it turns out, the time when we are closest to our most raw and untapped potential.

It is important to understand that you were born with a Genius Spark that still exists within you, even if it may be hidden. This spark can be reignited and coaxed into a warmth that illuminates your path, guides others in your orbit, and creates a meaningful, positive impact on the world around you. This Genius Spark is based on a unique set of traits that are etched into our brains through networks of neurons. These traits become our defaults, our go-to strategies for navigating the world. For instance, one person might naturally be inclined to categorize things. This alone isn't remarkable, but when combined with the ability to synthesize large amounts of information, it can make that person incredible at understanding and simplifying complex concepts. Another individual might be naturally inclined to communicate through stories, which can make them exceptional at building relationships. The traits themselves aren't the Genius Spark; the way they are applied is what's truly remarkable.

Over time, the unique traits that were designed to make us stand out get worn down by life and polished to fit within institutional, social, and family norms. In many cases, we become poorly-defined and ill-fitting copies of the people we were supposed to be. The truth is, we were all meant to be originals. When people are true to themselves, we describe them as authentic. *The Genius Spark* is designed to help you identify, clarify, regain, and validate your natural genius and inborn nature, to reclaim your authentic, one-of-a-kind self.

Often, the term 'genius' refers to someone endowed with extraordinary mental superiority. For our purposes, a genius is simply a person whose natural talents, skills, and passions are so effortlessly intertwined that they leave onlookers in awe, thinking, "Wow! How do they do it?" We all have the capacity to experience this synchronicity, but to access it requires attention, repetition, and a process. That's why this book exists. I'm convinced of the importance of this process. The reason I'm so passionate about it is that I've seen the positive change it can bring. I've seen how aligning our natural abilities with our purpose in life has the power to transform a person.

Unleashing the Genius Spark: Rekindling the Passion

Imagine seeing what was happening in your five-year-old brain, or is happening in your forty-five-year-old brain, and understanding where the genius was hiding. Psychometric assessments, which are commonly used by many organizations for professional development, are an accessible way to see inside the brain. These tests, (such as StrengthsFinder, Meyers Briggs, DISC or Enneagram) are often referred to as 'personality tests,' and they are designed to help individuals identify their natural talents and abilities, behavioral styles, personal attitudes, and inclinations. If used correctly, they can uncover our childhood potential and provide a map for unleashing it. Instead of searching in the dark, guessing about your why, switching careers, buying a motorcycle, and disrupting life to search for your Holy Grail, psychometric tests provide a clear starting point. And the Genius Spark can give you the opportunity to maximize what you learn from the results. As amazing as these tools are, however, the information alone does not unlock your potential or lead to fulfillment and happiness. The results simply remove the fog of wondering where to start or the excuse to settle for a safe but quiet discontentment. A good assessment will help you identify key traits which help you understand your individual worth and allow you to start living your true identity immediately.

After you take an assessment, you have two choices. Option one: You can file the results away as an interesting artifact and return to your life. Too many people do exactly that, putting their folder or printout in a file at work and never thinking about it again, despite continuing to feel the same old frustrations with their job and their life. Or, option two: You can use the results to paint a portrait of your genius potential. Using that picture as a guide to reassembling your life's story, you will experience a transformation as you start to notice your genius traits and how they can positively impact your life. For many, the transformation takes place gradually over thousands of micro-decisions. Then one day, when looking back, it will be hard to imagine the person you've become. I've seen it over and over in other people and experienced the transformation myself.

Like Rachel looking at her family's Wall of Fame, we know we can't go back to high school, return to our childhood, or recover paradise lost. But it's not too late to reclaim the magic, the Genius Spark, we once had. Granted, it's hard to gain a sense of direction without first remembering and realizing what is possible. What's possible is the ability and opportunity to tap into your true self and reach your potential, to reignite that Genius Spark that once made you feel invincible. The genius traits that inspired you and impressed others when you were young are still within you, just waiting to be released.

Awakening the Hidden Potential within Us

Taking our collective experiences into account, we'll move through the coming chapters, unfolding the mystery of our personal genius that often lies forgotten, dormant, and untapped within us. This journey will challenge the ideas of 'normal' and 'exceptional' that we have constructed in our minds, ideas that are dictated and influenced by societal conventions and expectations. The path is about understanding that every single one of us has the capacity to break free from the mold and carve our own unique path to excellence—be it in academics, sports, interpersonal relations, or life's pursuits post-graduation. The most important yardstick of achievement, we will discover, is the one we define ourselves. Through this exploration, we aim to awaken the 'better-than-average' trait that an inspirational teacher spotted in me many years ago—the Genius Spark that has enabled me to succeed and the genius traits that lie within each of us, waiting for their moment of revelation. So now, let's prepare to take the plunge into our first chapter, "Waking Up the Genius," and set out on this journey of self-discovery and personal excellence.

Key Lessons from the Introduction

1. **Inner Potential:** Everyone has the capacity to be exceptional in their own unique way.
2. **Recognition of One's Abilities:** Often, we are blind to our own potential, and it requires an external trigger or influence to make us realize our inherent abilities.
3. **Aspiration for Excellence:** Striving to be exceptional doesn't always mean being the best in everything; it's about being the best version of yourself.
4. **Self-Reflection and Growth:** Personal development is a journey of self-reflection and a continuous learning process to understand oneself better.
5. **Unlocking Hidden Genius:** Every individual possesses a unique genius within them. Recognizing and cultivating it can lead to a fulfilling and successful life.
6. **Empowerment through Personal Stories:** Personal stories and experiences can be powerful tools for inspiration and motivation, offering valuable personal and professional development insights.

Chapter 1

Awakening to the Extraordinary

I didn't realize that Mr. Roubidoux was standing right behind me. I was kidding around with a few classmates, and when I turned around, he put his hands on my shoulders, pushed me against the lockers, and lifted me into the air. My 4'8", eighty-three-pound body went limp in fear.

"Miller, you've got too much going for you to see it go to waste. I'm going to ride your tail for the rest of the year."

Mr. Roubidoux was tough; because of that, he was the most sought-after 8th-grade homeroom teacher by parents at South Junior High. Mom's active role in the PTA got me a seat in one of his classes. He knew I was an Eagle Scout. I was among the youngest to achieve that rank in Illinois and was the first Eagle he'd taught. Mr. Roubidoux was also a former Strategic Air Commander, and my accomplishments earned his respect, for about six weeks.

I had three big problems. Mr. Roubidoux randomly called on students to recite a part of the lesson from memory or provide an answer to a question, and it seemed like I always choked. I would try all of the tactics I knew not to be called on, like sitting in the back of the class and keeping my head down, and I still got called. Each time, I went tongue-tied. I was a very slow reader, dating back to early elementary school. I was sent to the reading lab and speech therapy every day to break the habit of sub-vocalizing words and help with my speech impediment. I got attention by being a jokester and instigator and was gifted at not getting caught, until 8th grade.

I wore my Boy Scout uniform with all of the badges one day a week. That was the school tradition. But my behavior as a goof-ball knucklehead created a stark contrast on a daily basis between the Eagle Scout image that I thought made me special and who I actually was.

Mr. Roubidoux tolerated it until I crossed the line. My dad purchased pepper spray, a new thing in 1968. I thought it would be "funny" to take it to school and spray it in the air in the stairwell and see what would happen when people passed through. A very knuckleheaded thing to do.

I also sprayed it in the corner of a White Hen Pantry convenience store. When I got home, the police were there. I denied it, gave them a good alibi, and they left. My dad knew otherwise but didn't say anything. After a few days, the guilt and paranoia that the police would find out led me to confess to Dad.

As I look back, Dad handled it brilliantly, although in a way that likely wouldn't fly today. He called the police station and concocted a scared-straight strategy. I was brought in, taken to a cell, and given a 3rd-degree interrogation by one of the officers. I broke down, cried, and pleaded for grace. The officer was stone-faced and simply got up, locked the cell, and left. I sat for over two hours and thought my life was about over. Dad and the officers were enjoying coffee and donuts and talking about their great job working me over.

Driving home, not a word was said. Dad never mentioned it to Mom and never brought it up again. But I learned later he told Mr. Roubidoux and enlisted him to get involved, too. That's why Mr. Roubidoux confronted me. He had a practice that if you messed up in class you were "invited" to return to his classroom after school for thirty minutes of heads-down work. No talking, no fidgeting—because if you did, he would say, "Miller: 30." That would mean an additional thirty minutes. If I attempted to plead my case? "Miller: another 30."

My inability to shut my mouth in class made me one of his most frequent after-school attendees. But I saw something I don't think other students picked up on. A couple times a week a young family would come to visit him with one or two kids in tow and say something like, "This is the man who changed my life." He profoundly changed mine too, but I wouldn't see those changes emerge until the end of high school and into college. I still saw others as having unique traits, being highly intelligent, articulate, athletic, bold, or interesting. By comparison I saw myself as a good sidekick but never a standout person on my own right. I borrowed from others' originality, and as Walt Disney said, "We have too many copies and not enough originals." I was one of those copies.

Chasing Exceptionality

From my time with Mr. Roubidoux, not to mention the police, my primary aspiration became clear: I yearned to rise above the sea of mediocrity, to shine as a beacon of excellence, and to be acknowledged for my unique talents. However, more often than not, I found myself settling somewhere in the vast middle ground. As a young man, I remained oblivious to the profound truth that each and every one of us possesses the capacity to become our own version of exceptional.

Caught in the relentless pursuit of this elusive exceptionalism, I closely observed those around me, meticulously crafting a mental checklist of the qualities required to transcend the boundaries of normalcy. Whether it was excelling in sports, forging meaningful connections within social circles, achieving academic brilliance, pursuing post-graduate endeavors, or carving out a

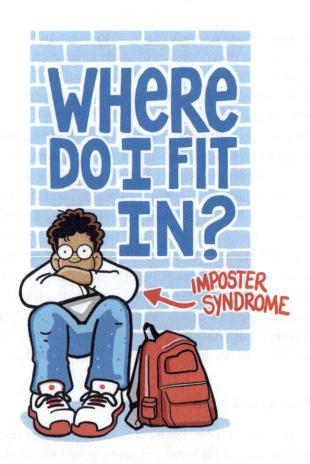

WHERE DO I FIT IN?

IMPOSTER SYNDROME

remarkable path beyond the confines of high school graduation, I believed there existed distinct avenues for achieving greatness. So, I pursued those things to varying degrees of success. In high school, I cruised through my coursework and played varsity tennis for a highly ranked school. However, no matter how successful I was in any particular area, the satisfaction of making it never lasted very long. Each time I reached a new accomplishment or achievement, I would lose steam. I was chasing excellence, but still it was excellence that I wasn't defining for myself.

Later, college was a new struggle. I was unaccustomed to the rigor and the challenges my professors presented me with, and I nearly failed a number of classes. I wasn't passionate about any major in particular so I ended up designing my own, covering everything from religion to technology. Graduation brought more questions than answers, and I progressed through a series of jobs, progress and setbacks, successes and failures, until a grand epiphany at the age of forty-five. Looking back, I realized my path contained several pivotal moments along the way to awakening my personal Genius.

Awakenings on the Path to Personal Genius

My first awakening happened at a camp in Colorado during high school. I was invited to go to a Fellowship of Christian Athletes camp and paid for by one of the Kraft family siblings. My adventure began in Estes Park, CO. As I stepped off the bus and into the Rocky Mountain wilderness, surrounded by college, Olympic, and professional athletes, I remember a feeling of gravity, like something BIG was going to happen while I was here. In my head, it was almost as if this experience was meant to confirm what I'd been suspecting up until this point: I was a pretty big deal.

Boy, was I wrong. I spent the camp outclassed and outgunned from almost every side. These elite athletes were in a stratosphere of achievement I hadn't even begun to contemplate. I had expected that being there would simply unlock the potential in me. Instead, I hit a wall, and doubt started swirling in my head. I was kidding myself about who I really was. I was a nominal athlete, and an average student who thought hanging around better people would rub off on me. There wasn't anything wrong with me, but I didn't feel particularly special, just average.

Experience and Introspection

It wasn't all bad, however. I don't know if it was the mountains, exhaustion from all the activities, or the voice in my head saying, "you have too much going for you for me to let it go to waste," but

I didn't leave the camp totally dejected. In fact, the experience had liberated something within me, giving me permission to be introspective, to start asking questions of myself, about myself. I didn't have a new burning mission or direction, but I felt different. The primary difference was that I had begun to become curious about my own life. A question simmered at the back of my mind:

"What is my life about?"

My second awakening came during my first real job, working as a project manager for Southwestern Bell, which is now AT&T. At Southwestern Bell I enrolled in three management courses to improve my manager capacity. The first course, Management By Objectives, dealt with setting norms for my team. I was taught to build a system in which we all spoke, acted, and operated with standardized intent, ensuring success by keeping everyone on the same path. But something didn't feel right.

The next course, Management by Exception, focused on "correcting non-standard performance." The course taught a system for identifying employee outliers and directing them back toward "our way" of doing things: the rules, the steps, and the decision ladder to get things done. Everything seemed designed to automate a process, removing any judgment or initiative. These courses reinforced the genius-killing instincts so common in our society.

Discovering the Power of Psychometric Assessments

The third course was an introduction to the DISC personality assessment. This was my first experience with psychometric assessments, and I latched on to that tool, giving it to everyone I knew and analyzing each one. People lit up when I shared the results of the DISC assessments. They were surprised at the accuracy; it was like a mirror, creating a word picture of what they looked like both on their best day and under pressure. The assessments connected dots, provided insights, and explained why they responded to experiences in predictable ways. They opened new opportunities to play to their purpose and their strengths. For me, these assessments presented a new focus, and as I became familiar with the words and phrases used to describe individual tendencies, my interest put me on a path I've followed for over 40 years.

Meeting Michael Vance: Unleashing Creativity and Authenticity

My third awakening came when I met Michael Vance, the former dean of Disney University. He was giving a workshop at a Haworth regional sales meeting in Dallas, and I was a new district manager who was discovering that often large companies want the same predictable process for sales. But Mike took a wrecking ball to that mindset.

He said nothing about sales; instead, he talked about what people are attracted to. He explained that most people spend their lives trying to imitate others, which is why we have many copies but few originals. This resonated with me deeply, as I had spent much of my life, without considerable success, trying to figure out how to be authentically myself while ALSO trying to live up to some socially constructed ideal.

At the time, I invested in every cassette training program Mike produced, each of which cost over $100 in the mid-1980s. It was a significant investment, but worth it. For many years, I set January aside to go through each of Vance's workshops, and every year I discovered new insights that became a part of me. Vance's content and style were so compressed and impactful that each year, I gained a new understanding of creativity that helped me to become a better leader and a more creative person. Vance exuded an infectious zest for life and believed that given the right conditions and environment, everyone could lean into their innate tendencies to create momentum, empower others, champion initiatives, and, perhaps most importantly, build their own versions of their best selves.

My work with the DISC tool had helped me discover what made people unique, and how they could identify their strengths. As I delved deeper into my quest to discover my own 'best self,' I discovered my journey was tied to helping others to define and seek their own best selves. My unique traits of thinking in themes and categories, wanting to achieve, having a constant desire for new knowledge, and making meaningful connections between disparate and apparently unrelated observations and facts, allowed me to support others in developing a vision of their own best selves. I began to coach and guide my clients through this lens.

Embracing Strengths: A Paradigm Shift

In 2001, a final realization came when I stumbled upon the book *Now, Discover Your Strengths*, which completely changed my understanding of the path to personal growth. The book, by Donald O. Clifton and Marcus Buckingham, described research about how our brains are wired and how the strongest and most intuitive parts of our brains represent what we naturally do best and enjoy most. In other words, our strengths. The authors argued that focusing on our strengths and not spending too much time on fixing our weaknesses was the key to unlocking our true potential.

I immediately took the book's assessment, called the "StrengthsFinder," and discovered my top five strengths: Strategic®, Achiever®, Relator®, Input®, and Learner®. The descriptions that accompanied these strengths gave me new language to rely upon as I talked about and reflected on my own abilities. I was naturally wired to see patterns, and this helped me when I started doing workshops to describe the interests and behaviors of participants. I would take a look at their strengths and make educated guesses about what they were like, which often turned out to be accurate. People started calling it my "magic trick."

CoreClarity:
Unveiling Patterns and Relationships

Even given all I was learning, it wasn't until 2005, when I met Candace Fitzpatrick, the managing partner for commercial real estate firm CRESA Partner, that I truly understood how to put my new-found knowledge into practice. Candace had just finished her master's degree studying StrengthsFinder and had developed a system called CoreClarity® to make it more accessible and practical. She grouped the strengths into four categories and gave each category a different color and memorable related phrases. The first time I saw my five strengths in CoreClarity's color system, the lightbulb went off. It was like having a deck of cards that showed the patterns and relationships between my strengths, making it easier for me to understand how they all fit together. Most importantly, it provided a shorthand to visualize patterns and relationships between strengths. It gave me an even better way to TALK about myself, and I knew I could help others discover the same.

I got certified to use the CoreClarity system with project teams and started doing workshops for free in my spare time to see if I was any good at it. And let me tell you, it was so much fun! My first paid engagement was a half-day workshop with eight people in 2006, and I earned $250. Fast forward 22 years, and I've trained or coached more than 19,000 people, using my magic trick to understand people's interests and habits by looking at their five strengths.

Looking back upon my life, I stand in awe of the many chapters that converged to form my unique story. Each success, each failure, and every moment of uncertainty served as essential brushstrokes, painting the portrait of my awakening. Within the chapters of our individual experiences, we uncover the power and potential of our personal genius, awaiting the day when we will fully embrace and manifest it in all its glory. The journey continues, and as I cast my gaze forward, I am filled with a renewed sense of purpose and an unwavering commitment to guide others in their own quest for self-discovery and the awakening of their brilliance.

The Forge of Experience: The Trial by Fire—FAA Training

In 2011, I was a senior partner at a consulting firm working with a variety of clients. I had tried several times unsuccessfully to bring the CoreClarity concept into my practice, but my colleagues weren't convinced. When a short notice engagement with the Federal Aviation Administration popped up, I saw an opportunity to bring the tools I was most excited about into fuller use. I'd be delivering a four-day training to a group of FAA employees from the Washington En-Route facility.

At this time, I had never done anything more than a day-long training with these materials. I had no idea how I was going to put together FOUR days' worth of training and content. But I was confident that if I could get this group engaged and excited about the concept of talking about their strengths, I would be able to move the needle with them.

Before I arrived, I took a look at an assessment document that summarized the group's makeup. Sixty-six percent of them had 'Deliberative' in their top five strengths, and 44 percent of them had 'Analytical.' For context, these concentrations are each over 400 percent higher than we'd expect, given national averages.

"Oh, man," I thought. "This isn't going to be easy."

Those two strengths combined typically result in a person who can list and define ALL of the reasons why each and every one of your ideas is not feasible, won't work, and is ultimately doomed to fail. And I would have a room full of these people.

When I walked into the training facility, the group had already arrived, sullenly seated around the edges of the room. There were patches of conversation here and there, small pockets of colleagues huddled together chatting, but the body language of almost everyone present gave off the same message: "This is going to be a waste of my time."

As I headed to the front of the room to set up my things, a man jested, "Are we so messed up that they had to send YOU?" Another quipped "So, you're going to FIX us, huh?" I shot back something noncommittal like, "Well, we will see!" and quickly busied myself with getting ready. I pulled out my cell phone and gave my managing partner a call. "Hey, is there something you didn't tell me about this group?" He chuckled and replied, "Well, you're currently in a room with the worst-performing group of employees in the entire FAA. Their officer is at a loss and basically told them they were going to spend four days with you 'getting fixed.' Do your best, their money's already been spent. Good luck."

After we hung up, I took a deep breath, and then another, and then I took my shot. "Alright everyone, let's go ahead and get started."

The group slowly shuffled over and moved their seats into loose rows. I began by passing out a simple handout— a list of strengths and their simple descriptions. While I handed out pages, one of the participants made a comment that has stuck *verbatim* in my head ever since: "Listen, we don't believe in any of this fuzzy-wuzzy, horiscopy, Kumbaya."

Everyone went quiet, waiting to see how I'd respond. I finished handing out the papers, took a deep breath, looked over the room, and asked, "What's the number one priority at the FAA?"

Silence.

"No, seriously," I went on, "What's your number one job?"

Someone spoke up from the back of the group: "Safety."

"Yup," I said. "At this point we haven't even *begun* this training, and you have no idea what I'm going to talk about. But I want you to take a look at the list in front of you. It's a list of strengths or talents people possess. If your job is to maintain safety, to mitigate risk and consider all potential threats, to understand all the ways in which something might go wrong, which one of these strengths *immediately* stands out to you as being incredibly useful?" I paused while they read through the list, hoping it would work.

"Deliberative," said a different voice, this time closer to the front of the room. I saw heads nodding in affirmation—they'd all identified the same strength.

I smiled.

"That's right. People with this talent are *exceptional* at anticipating and planning for obstacles. I cannot imagine a more useful skill in your line of work. And guess what? Sixty-six percent of the people in this room not only have that talent, but it's up at the top of the list of things they're naturally good at."

I could see their faces had begun to shift from mistrust to curiosity. I hadn't won them over yet, but we were close. "So let me ask you something else. Look at that description of 'Deliberative' again: 'Every risk is identified and every potential disaster is imagined.' Now, how might that get in your way?"

It was clear from the uncomfortable glances that they could see where I was going, so I plowed ahead. "I'll bet before I even walked into the room, most of y'all had come up with a pretty solid list of all the ways in which this experience would probably be a waste of your time. And guess what? I don't blame you. It's literally in your nature. I'm not here to change you or force you into any 'Kumbaya BS.' I'm here to help you see yourself better, so that the things you do naturally can benefit you instead of making you miserable."

I saw folks glancing at each other to see where the general sentiment was, so I took another small gamble. "I'll make you a deal. My company's already been paid, so it really doesn't matter to me how this goes. But if you give me half a day's honest effort, and you still think this is garbage, I'll pack up and leave."

It worked.

For the next four days, we listed, analyzed, discussed, and dissected each of their top talents. By the end, I don't think they were "fixed," but they left with calm demeanors, a sense of hope, and a sneaking suspicion that work might not HAVE to be a miserable experience for them.

> ## *"We must be willing to get rid of the life we've planned, so as to have the life that is waiting for us."*
>
> ## *- Joseph Campbell*

So, Now What?

My work has brought me in contact with a myriad of different people. The vast majority of the clients I've worked with and others I've observed can be described similarly to myself before my awakenings. They're just like Rachel from the introduction of this book. They operate largely within the confines of what might be considered normal. They experience momentary but mostly unrepeatable moments of concentrated genius, and they often ask themselves the same questions I had been asking myself.

The Three Exceptions

I have, however, run into three kinds of exceptions:

First, those who deliberately defy norms in an unhealthy and unproductive way. They let their unique talents turn into dominating quirks that are off-putting and awkward to work with. There is a spectrum of reasons, from a lack of self-awareness to a desire to play the rebel to authentic sensory challenges.

The second exception is savants, true one-offs who are so incomparable, they have little to teach or impart. For these people—often incredible athletes, natural musicians, or mathematical geniuses—their abilities are not related to a regular application of a unique trait but rather result from a *massive* concentration of ability, such as physical prowess or raw intellectual capacity.

The third exception is people like Mike Vance, the man whose seminars were transformative experiences for me. He was the catalyst for my understanding of creativity, originality, and genius. The innate abilities of people like him are so powerfully expressed and so deeply aligned with their purposes in the world that when they are doing what they do best, it often looks like *magic*. The thing about magic is that, whether or not our inner child wants to admit it, there is a secret behind how it works. If they wanted to, the magician could pull back the curtain and explain it to you. Personally, I like the mystery, so I'm content not having a magician reveal these secrets. However, people are a completely different story. When it comes to people, I became driven to unlock the secret to the magic. I wanted to know: Was it possible that all of us could live into our own exceptional traits, as people like Vance had?

Unlocking the Secret to Personal Magic

What I've found is that the answer is yes: It is possible to (re) discover your Genius Spark, and to wield it deliberately. It's not automatic, and it takes intentional effort. In fact, I've found that three key elements must be present for someone to consistently live into their spark. These elements build on one another in cycles of 'meaning making' and discovery and ultimately lead to a capacity to call upon and direct your Genius Spark whenever it is necessary. It's like having a roadmap for your own personal success. Taken in tandem, **Language + Insight + Energy = Magic**.

1. **Language:** "A picture is worth a thousand words." When it comes to knowing yourself, a succinct description of your key traits and tendencies is worth even more. That's why it's important to create what I like to think of as your "Genius Portrait."

2. **Insight:** Once you've got your Genius Portrait, what do you do with it? This is where the real magic happens. By continually reflecting on your portrait, you'll gain a deeper understanding of yourself and how you fit into the world around you.

3. **Energy:** Finally, when you have a clear picture and understanding of your Genius Portrait, you will discover where you should focus your energy. You'll be able to zero in on the things that bring you joy and help bring you into a state of *flow*, rather than *drain* you of your energy.

In this book, I'll first provide scientific and experiential evidence that supports the Genius Spark system. Then, I'll walk you through constructing, considering, and acting upon your Genius Portrait. Finally, I'll flesh out the implications of the Genius Spark and set the stage for what I think comes next. Over the last 20 years, all my clients are either searching for or developing what makes them unique. Most people I've worked with grew up like I did, within a constellation of norms to which they conformed with varying degrees of personal success, fulfillment, and happiness. But the real journey begins with discovering, or rediscovering, who you were born to be.

The best time to start is now, so let's get moving.

As we embark on this exploration of the Genius Spark, it is essential to recognize the untamed brilliance we possessed in our early years. We were all geniuses once, effortlessly absorbing information, discovering the world with wide-eyed wonder, and expressing our unique gifts through play and imagination. But as time passes and we navigate

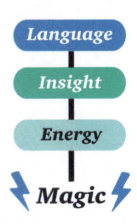

the complexities of adulthood, that innate magic can fade, buried beneath the weight of responsibilities and societal expectations. However, it doesn't have to remain lost. The power to reconnect with our childlike brilliance lies within each of us. We have the capacity to tap into our Genius Spark intentionally, reigniting the flames of creativity, innovation, and limitless potential. Let us now unravel the mysteries that hold the key to reclaiming our innate genius, rediscovering the seeds planted at our birth, and unlocking the path to mastery.

Key Lessons from Chapter One: Waking Up the Genius

1. **Recognize the potential within yourself:** Discover the exceptional qualities and talents that others may see in you, even when you don't recognize them in yourself.

2. **Embrace curiosity and introspection:** Allow yourself to be curious about your life, asking deeper questions to uncover your purpose and meaning.

3. **Awakenings shape your path:** Reflect on pivotal moments and experiences that have led to personal growth and self-discovery, acknowledging their importance in your journey.

4. **Tap into your unique strengths:** Identify and leverage your strengths using tools like psychometric assessments and self-reflection to gain insights and make meaningful connections.

5. **Understand the power of language:** Develop a clear and concise description of your key traits and tendencies to better articulate and understand yourself.

6. **Cultivate insight through reflection:** Continually reflect on your strengths and characteristics, gaining a deeper understanding of yourself and your place in the world.

7. **Direct your energy toward what brings you joy:** Use your newfound self-awareness to focus on activities and pursuits that align with your strengths and values, bringing you fulfillment and a flow state.

8. **Begin the journey of self-discovery now:** Explore your unique qualities and uncover your genius, understanding that the best time to begin is in the present moment.

Chapter 2

Reigniting the Spark

"Don't ever let somebody tell you can't do something. Not even me. You got a dream, you gotta protect it. When people can't do something themselves, they're gonna tell you that you can't do it. You want something, go get it. Period."

Chris Gardner—The Pursuit of Happiness

Nurturing Early Signs: Unveiling the Genius Spark in Childhood

I feel fortunate that my wife, Lisa, and I noticed some of our kids' genius traits very early. Even as young as three years old, our daughter Michelle was a risk taker, motivated strongly by connections with others and the world around her. As a toddler, whenever she saw a new kid in front of our house, she would run down the sidewalk excitedly to greet her newfound friend with a hug.

Our son Nathan looked at things differently, even as a young child. When Nathan was a toddler, he once thought Lisa had given Michelle three pancakes for breakfast and only two to him. There was a third underneath that he didn't see, and his keen sense of fairness erupted. He got up, took his plate, and threw it in the trash, accusing mom of short-shifting him and favoring his older sister. We never forgot his hilarious tirade of righteous indignation, knowing it could be an asset and a strength. In elementary school, he became a champion for underdogs, protecting them from being bullied and becoming their loyal friend.

Order and discipline were traits we noticed in Tyler from the time he ate in a highchair. He made sure none of the foods touched, separating the peas from the mashed potatoes and ensuring the gravy did not intrude. As he grew older he loved complex stories and plots, like *Harry Potter* and *Lord of the Rings*. When we told him that if he wanted to be homeschooled he'd need to learn an instrument, his discipline and deep reflection got channeled into piano and composition.

Each of my children has since grown up, and even today I see their original Genius in the variety of ways they approach the world and the myriad beliefs they hold about their places within it. However, my children don't manifest their Genius all day, every day. Michelle, Nathan, and Tyler experience their educational and professional environments in much the same way the vast majority experience theirs: with a combination of boredom, fatigue and mental exhaustion that's briefly and infrequently interrupted by moments of serendipitous brilliance. Those brief moments are when they are most authentically themselves.

The Fading Flame: Challenges of Lost Genius Spark

Robert Greene, a best-selling author and popular speaker, took an incredibly circuitous route to his career in writing and motivational speaking. By his estimate, he worked more than 50 jobs throughout his life, including being a construction worker and translator. In his book *Mastery* he reminds us, "At your birth, a seed is planted. The seed is your uniqueness . . . you have a destiny to fulfill. The stronger you feel and maintain it—as a force, a voice, or in whatever form—the greater the chance for fulfilling this Life's Task and achieving mastery."

"What holds people back from learning and mastery is not inability or lack of capacity, but instead it is *impatience.*"

- Robert Greene

Greene is correct on the special nature of each individual human being. Considering all the possibilities of qualities and personality traits, the one thing we can be certain of is that of all the billions of people in the world, there is no one specifically like us. And that is our special gift. Most people start out strong, knowing who they are and what they like. During that magical period from three until they enter school at five, kids "experience the wonder of the world in a way that they never will experience again in their lifetime. This is the age of imagination, of magic, of play."[2]

These moments of brilliance are what I am interested in, and they bring up in me a series of key questions we must tackle before we can move toward making magic on purpose: What allows children to so naturally access and leverage their Genius Spark? Where does our Genius Spark go as we age, and how can we tell it's being hidden? How are people impacted when their Genius Spark is hidden? What about when it's unleashed? And perhaps most importantly, what should we do now?

I would like to suggest that many of the tendencies children exhibit around creativity are the same tendencies that, if projected forward, would allow adults to more frequently, and more

---

2. "The Magical Age," *Simply Parenting*, April 1, 2007, bit.ly/3ATTpjz.

intentionally, tap into their Genius Spark. Dr. Tiffany Kimbrough, associate professor and pediatrician at Children's Hospital of Richmond at VCU, knows the power of that intuitive childhood ability to simply learn and grow. She tells parents they will be amazed at how quickly their young children absorb information, something new parents learn quickly. Kimbrough explains how "five-year-olds are like sponges and are constantly learning."[3]

When I am leading a training and ask an audience, "Do you remember some of that five-year-old magic?" almost every hand goes up. Yet when I follow up by asking, "Does that magic get you up in the morning? Do you still feel it in your adult life and in your jobs?" The hands remain in their laps. They all know they had it once, and they all feel remorse at how easily it was lost. However, it doesn't have to be that way, and it's the job of every adult to remember how brilliant they were as a child. The most creative and innovative minds recognize this, as people like George Land and Sir Ken Robinson knew. As Pablo Picasso said about his genius, "It took me four years to paint like Raphael, but a lifetime to paint like a child."

Childlike Wonder: Unlocking the Genius Spark Within

Let's examine what we can learn about the Genius Spark from kids. Although each of us has this Spark within us, it is most evident and easily observed in children. The Genius Spark is a person's innate ability to leverage their unique outlooks, abilities, and patterns of thought in order to positively influence themselves, others, and the world around them. It is a deeply-rooted curiosity, a unique way of thinking, persistent passion, and creative engagement with the world. The Genius Spark is the vibrant energy released when you express your unique mix of natural talents and creative thinking,

---

3. Amy Morin, LCSW, and Wendy Wisner, "5-Year-Old Child Development Milestones," *Verywell Family*, February 3, 2022, www.verywellfamily.co m/5-year-old-developmental-milestones-620713.

and when purposefully channeled, it can lead to extraordinary achievements. This radiant energy not only motivates you but also inspires others around you. As Land's research tells us, children naturally and intuitively access their Genius Spark in nearly everything they do, and it's helpful to recall how, as children, we all did that too.

Children are willing to engage in repeated trial and error to pursue a specific goal or outcome. A child attempting to reach a jar of cookies on a high shelf will try several strategies to acquire the cookies, many of which might not work immediately. They might use a stool to climb onto the countertop only to find they still cannot reach the jar. They might recruit the services of an older brother or sister as a co-conspirator, only to find them unwilling or unavailable to help. They might even fashion some type of extendable poking device out of wire coat hangers and duct tape, eventually allowing them to garner their sweet prize. The point isn't whether they achieve their goal; the outcome is immaterial, though delicious. The important thing is the confidence and creativity the child employed and willingness to try again after failing. This common adaptive behavior of children demonstrates a willingness to explore options until the 'right' one presents itself. There are several intrinsic qualities of childhood that enable children to effortlessly pursue their interests and find joy in their days.

Children rapidly develop, integrate, and apply 'soft skills' such as cooperation, communication, and compromise. Children are naturally social creatures; as they grow, they learn to interact with others in their environment. They learn to communicate their needs and desires, to listen to others, and to work together to achieve a common goal—all of these are key components of the Genius Spark. Children's ability to quickly develop and apply these soft skills allows them to navigate the world around them more effectively, making it easier for them to achieve their goals.

Children instinctively pursue things that stimulate them. Their natural interests give rise to their natural talents because they allow themselves to be awed and absorbed in the activities or subjects that draw their attention. Children have a natural curiosity and a desire to explore and understand the world around them. As they engage in these activities, they develop a deeper understanding and move toward mastery. This is how natural talents emerge.

Children are inherently courageous and haven't developed any problematic mental models about how the world works or where they fit within it. Children are fearless and unafraid to take risks. They are willing to try new things and explore the unknown. They have yet to run into obstacles that challenge how they see the world or make them question who they are within it. This natural courage allows them to take on new challenges, push themselves to their limits, and ultimately seek meaningful goals.

What Happens to that Spark?

As we age, it becomes more likely our Genius Spark will be obscured, hidden, or ignored. The reasons have to do with our modern culture, the natural course of mental and emotional development, and the collection of systems and institutions we have built that prioritize efficiency over humanity. George Land lists the following forces that diminish our original creativity and genius:

1. **Socialization:** Our creativity is often suppressed as we grow up and conform to social norms and expectations.
2. **Education:** Our educational system emphasizes memorization of information and the repetition of conventional methods, which stifle creativity.
3. **Perception:** Our perceptions of reality limit our creative abilities, causing us to see the world in a narrow and rigid way.

4. **Experience:** Repetition of the same experiences and exposure to only a narrow range of information limit our creativity.

5. **Responsibility:** The increasing responsibilities of adulthood, such as work and family obligations, limit our time and resources for pursuing creative outlets.

6. **Pressure:** Pressure to conform to expectations and perform to a high standard limit our ability to take risks and experiment with new ideas. [4]

Brené Brown, an esteemed research professor, author, and speaker, has spent her career studying the factors that motivate and inhibit people from achieving personal success. Brown believes in encouraging people to give active voice to their internal monologues. Her well-known catchphrase is, "The story I'm telling myself." Whereas Brown typically employs this phrase interpersonally, it can be useful to assess the stories we are telling ourselves *about* ourselves. Saying it out loud gives people an opportunity to objectively assess the likelihood of that story being the truth, and opens the door to the potential veracity of a second story.

Just as each of us possesses a one-of-a-kind combination of interests and talents, our individual experiences lead us to craft a unique narrative about how we think the world works, and describes the space that we occupy within it. The problem with internal narratives is that they seldom consider the whole picture, and they can often poison the impressions we have of our own capacity and the capacity of others. So, what are some of these problematic narratives, and what systems and structures encourage their development?

---

4. George Land, *Breakpoint and Beyond: Mastering the Future Today* (New York: Harper-Collins, 1998).

I'm only good if I'm successful.

Some people only focus on the outcome and not the value of the effort. This *fixed mindset* can limit our potential, preventing us from trying again and learning from failure. Even in parenting my own children, I've noticed a tendency in myself to celebrate what they have DONE, rather than the skills, strategies, or effort they employed in order to do it. On the flip side, praising effort rather than results can lead to a *growth mindset* where we see opportunity even in failures. It's important to remember success is not the only thing that matters—effort, growth, resiliency, and being true to ourselves are important, too. Those with the Genius Spark know this.[5]

---

5. Carol S. Dweck, *Mindset: The New Psychology of Success* (New York: Ballantine Books, 2016).

If I don't measure up, I should try something else.

We live in a world where people, ideas, and products are constantly judged and evaluated. But sometimes, this focus on evaluating everything can make us believe we aren't good enough, preventing us from seeing our own Genius Spark and all of our skills and habits that can help us achieve our goals. If students are evaluated solely on test scores, ignoring their effort, creativity, relationships, or classroom contributions, they might feel inadequate and abandon their passions.

There's no time for fun; we have work to do.

Unfortunately, this idea is too common in our education system and in many professional environments. In reality, play is crucial for creativity and innovation. Studies have shown that play can improve memory, decrease stress, and help us connect with our true selves.

For example, let's look at the field of improvised music. Musician and researcher Dr. Charles Limb conducted a study on jazz musicians and found that during improvisation, the part of the brain responsible for planned actions and self-censoring showed a slowdown in activity. This means the musicians could shut down impulses that might block their flow of new ideas, leading to a clear path for spontaneous thought that developed over years of practice.[6]

The takeaway? Don't be afraid to take some time to play and have fun. It's essential to unlocking your Genius Spark. When playfulness is discouraged, on the other hand, it can lead to stagnation and a lack of creativity. In a work environment where employees are always expected to be serious and professional, for example, they may feel uncomfortable suggesting unique and creative ideas.

---

6. Michael Sigman, "The Importance of Play: It's More Than Just Fun and Games," HuffPost, https://www.huffpost.com/entry/play-importance_b_821238

It's much better to fit in than to stand out.

Society often expects us to act, talk, and think in a particular way. This can limit our creativity and ability to think outside the box. In school, if teachers only accept one approach to arriving at an answer, it stops students from exploring creative and unique solutions.

To counter this stifling conformity, we must cultivate an open and inquisitive mindset when engaging with people who possess distinctive perspectives or personalities. It's natural to feel hesitant or doubtful when encountering those who think, communicate, or behave differently. However, the key to unlocking our true potential lies in embracing curiosity. Individuals who deviate from the norm or think unconventionally may be perceived as odd or out of place. Rather than stifling our growth, we ought to celebrate and welcome diverse ideas and approaches.

Forces That Crush Our Genius

Breaking the Chains:
Overcoming Limiting Beliefs

The concepts I'm describing shouldn't surprise you. A global economy, emergent technologies, widening income inequality, and a laser focus on results, outcomes, and profits all create an environment that is *not* focused on rewarding someone's Genius Spark. As a result, our experiences at work and at home tend to leave us with low energy and lower hope. Situations where we are not actively employing our strongest natural talents can leave us drained rather than invigorated.

If you're a manager or supervisor, statistics show that since the pandemic, only 20 percent of employees put their heart and soul into their work and service. Another 30 percent are CAVE dwellers—"Consistently Against Virtually Everything." According to Gallup,[7] the other 50 percent of the workforce will do a good job if you tell them what to do and how to do it. Then you must follow up to make sure they did it. They are "the managed." You get part of their brains and none of their passion.

If you add the 30 percent of toxic employees to the 50 percent who only do what they're told, you'll realize you spend too much time babysitting 80 percent of your team. Without understanding how your team members are wired and what they need, your responsibility as a manager to grow, improve, and inspire others will drain you of energy, rather than filling you with purpose and direction. However, work and life do not have to be that way.

Top performers—the 20 percent—have one thing in common: They regularly tap into their most dominant talents. In other words, their activities and efforts are directly aligned with the things they are naturally wired to be good at. They are energized, positive, focused, and highly engaged. And they infect

---

7. Gallup, *State of the Global Workplace: 2021 Report* (Washington, D.C.: Gallup, Inc., 2021), https://www.gallup.com/workplace/349484/state-of-the-global-workplace-report -2021.aspx.

everyone around them. That's why they're sought out. On the other side are those whose lives do not frequently draw upon their natural talents and abilities. The following is a sampling of the most common things clients say when I ask why they're coming to me to chat about their lives and careers:

- "I'm successful, but I don't know why I am so tired and stressed all the time."
- "Why do I feel like all I do is put out fires every day?"
- "I've tried a dozen self-help programs. Why hasn't anything clicked yet?"
- "I feel stuck or trapped and don't know what to do."
- "I feel guilty that my family always comes in second and has to compete with my job."
- "Why do I think happiness is always around the next corner?"
- "I feel like I'm being held back (by my peers, my boss, my company, my family)."
- "If people could only see what I'm truly capable of doing, I'd feel respected and happy."
- "I feel alone, and there is no one there to help me."
- "Why am I commuting two hours a day?"
- "Do I really like what I'm doing?"
- "Wow, look at what I've been missing: dinner with the family, attending my daughter's soccer games, and, well, you can fill in the blank."

These refrains mirror what research suggests about the quality of every aspect of our lives if we are not afforded the opportunity to align what we're doing with what we're naturally good at. The impacts span the personal and the professional, and include rather alarming implications for mental and physical health outcomes. Conversations with clients have repeatedly convinced me that one of our primary sources of suffering as humans stems from repeatedly engaging in pursuits that are misaligned with our greatest assets and values as individuals.

It's Never Too Late: Landau's Extraordinary Transformation

The TV show *America's Got Talent* attracts millions of viewers each season. They are all eager to see who is the next diamond in the rough. And, if we're honest, we also look forward to the train wrecks, those cases where ambition exceeds strength.

On June 22, 2011, a 36-year-old man who worked as a new car detailer—basically a car washer—from Logan, West Virginia, was the last contestant to audition. In the pre-audition interview, he said, "I've washed so many cars . . . I've been up to here in bubbles. Now it's time to go somewhere else."

He walked confidently onto the stage dressed in a sports coat and jeans, sporting long dreadlocks and chewing gum. He laughed as he pointed at Howie Mandel, one of the judges. Another judge, Piers Morgan, asked, "Why are you laughing?" The contestant gushed that he had loved Howie ever since he heard him do his comedy character "Little Bobbie." He then gave his imitation of Little Bobbie. When asked for his name, he replied, somewhat formally, "Landau Eugene Murphy, Jr."

"Landau, are you chewing gum?" asked Morgan.

"Yes, I am," Landau replied, innocently laughing.

"I wouldn't do that when you're performing in the show," Morgan told him. "Seriously." So, Landau promptly took the gum out of his mouth and placed it in the front pocket of his jeans. The crowd roared with laughter.

When Sharon Osbourne, the third judge, asked what he intended to do for the audition, Landau said, "I do all kinds of music, but tonight I'm just here to pursue my dream." The judges, the audience, and the viewers were all certain they were about to witness an absolute train wreck of epic proportions. But when the music began—a big-band soundtrack right out of the 1950s—Landau pulled the mic to his lips and belted out a stunning rendition of the Sinatra classic "I've Got You Under My Skin." Heads jerked up to see if what they were hearing was really coming out of Landau: a deep, mellow baritone voice. His tone was resonant, his phrasing was captivating. He was more Sinatra than Sinatra. Sharon Osbourne stood up in the middle of the song and began to clap to the rhythm. Cameras panned the audience, picking up the open-mouthed astonishment.

That night we all saw a quintessential fairy tale unfolding in real time on network TV. The music ended in a huge ovation. As the audience quieted down, Osbourne asked, "Was there a tape playing? Were you miming?" Morgan, visibly stunned, asked if Landau had ever auditioned before: "Never in my life. First-ever audition in front of anybody."

The moment was overwhelming. It certainly was for Landau. It was for me, too. I've shown the audition clip at several of our training sessions; inevitably, people in the room begin to wipe their eyes. Landau was also moved. In tears, he said, "I never knew they would love me like that!" He never knew. How could a talent like Landau Eugene Murphy, Jr., remain invisible for 36 years of his life? Why did his performance touch a nerve in everyone? Could I experience a similar rush of exhilaration in the things I do? Who am I overlooking? Am I missing a diamond in the rough?

We are all like Landau. We instinctively know there is something extraordinary about us. Few of us experience an opportunity to create a platform for our artistry or leadership. But Landau just walked out before the whole world in confidence and gave his best. Morgan was right when he said, "You have a natural, God-given talent." So was Mandel, who told Landau, "Your life is never going to be the same." Now, before going on to the next chapter, take the time to watch the video. See what the Genius Spark looks like in one incredible man.

Late-Blooming Brilliance:
It's Never Too Late to Ignite Your Genius Spark

I'm considered a late bloomer at sixty-eight. I reinvented my business in the last two years, finishing this book and a web app that supports it. My wife and I signed up for a 20-year project buying a historical 19-acre ranch that needs lots of love to turn into a retreat facility. In the evening, we sometimes look at each other and wonder, "What are we thinking?" Every week greets us with setbacks, big mountains we need to climb, and questions like, "Is this going to work?" We are in over our heads, and all of this may crash and burn, but every day we wake up eager, with a sense of purpose and the energy that comes from playing to our strengths.

It's not too late for you or me. The NASA research is clear. Unless our Genius Spark ignites by the time we are teenagers, it fades to a flicker by adulthood. Distractions, emotional numbness, and regrets replace the dreams of what might have been. Most people eventually settle and make peace with the available choices.

But it doesn't have to be that way. Like me, many leaders did not discover their best self until late in life. Henry Ford didn't become a successful auto manufacturer until he was 45 years old. Ray Kroc was 59 when he bought his first MacDonald's. Laura Ingalls Wilder published her first book, *Little House in the Big Woods*, the basis for the Little House on the Prairie series, when she was 65. And the great American painter, Anna Mary Robertson Moses, better known as "Grandma Moses," didn't even start painting until she was 78.

According to an old Chinese proverb, "The best time to plant an oak tree was twenty years ago. The second-best time is today."

Igniting the Flame Within: Embracing Our Authenticity and Reshaping Our Destiny

The pursuit of rediscovering and nurturing our Genius Spark is a lifelong odyssey, one that holds the power to redefine our existence. It matters not whether we awaken to our innate talents early in life or find them later along our path. The crux of the journey lies in the profound realization of our unique abilities, the embrace of our passions, and the unwavering commitment to align our actions with our intrinsic strengths.

Through the awe-inspiring tale of Landau Eugene Murphy Jr., the emergence of late-blooming leaders, and the defiant spirits of artists who shattered expectations, we glean a resounding truth: It is never too late to delve into the depths of our concealed potential and craft a life steeped in purpose and fulfillment. Each of these narratives serves as a beacon of hope, illuminating the dormant embers within us, urging us to ignite our Genius Spark and radiate our brilliance upon the world.

Let this be etched in our hearts as we stand at the precipice of transformation: The optimal time to ignite our Genius Spark may have passed in the corridors of yesteryears, but the second-best time, the time we hold in our hands today, brims with limitless possibilities. Let's embark on this extraordinary journey, guided by the light of authenticity, as we unravel the extraordinary depths of our being and forge a destiny that harmonizes with our innate genius. With every step forward, let's unleash the brilliance that has slumbered within us, cascading ripples of inspiration, and leaving an indelible mark upon the tapestry of existence.

Key Lessons for Chapter Two: Reigniting the Spark

1. **The "Genius Spark":** Refers to an individual's unique talents, experiences, and potential.
2. **Childhood Creativity:** Children naturally tap into their Genius Spark, exhibiting creativity, curiosity, and a willingness to explore.
3. **Never Too Late:** It's never too late to discover and nurture your Genius Spark, as exemplified by stories of late-blooming leaders and artists.
4. **Obstacles to Expression:** Societal norms, educational systems, and personal narratives can obscure or hinder the expression of the Genius Spark.
5. **Alignment with Talents:** Aligning actions with your natural talents, passions, and strengths is essential for living a life of purpose and fulfillment.
6. **Transformation and Authenticity:** Embarking on a transformative journey, embracing authenticity, and unlocking your brilliance can lead to a more fulfilling life.
7. **Now is the Time:** The best time to ignite your Genius Spark may have been in the past, but the second-best time is always today.

Chapter 3

Breaking the Cycle

"The seed that we planted in this man's mind may change everything."

—Cobb from the film *Inception*

Our U-shaped table arrangement allowed me to make eye contact with everyone in the training session. Everyone, that is, except Bob. He sat in the corner of the room, slouched, his arms folded. His message was clear: "Leave me alone. Whatever you're selling, I'm not buying."

Honestly, I wasn't sure anyone in the room was buying. This management team from a 55,000-person organization—staff managers, operations managers, and the executives who oversaw both groups—had been told they needed to learn how to work together. The Boss had ordered them to go to my four-day off-site retreat and return "fixed." The not-so-subtle negative message from the top wasn't helping my case. Most people in the group were cordial, even curious. But not Bob; his mind was made up. No navel-gazing, Kumbaya, touchy-feely, psycho-babble stuff for him. The morning session introduced the case for strengths-based leadership and highlighted some strengths and natural talents in the room. Then we tried an exercise:

Make a list of those things you do at work that energize you, AND then list the things that make you feel drained (as you do them or even think about them).

The room warmed up, and most people freely volunteered examples of both. Although the group dumped a lot of frustration and despair down "the drain," lights started coming on for several participants. It's powerful to acknowledge that some things help us gain energy, and others drain it from us.

But Bob sat, arms folded, studying the third button on his shirt.

When we broke for lunch, everyone went in different directions. The last three people in the room were Jim, a colleague and a clinical psychologist from my firm, Bob, and me. Since no one from Bob's organization wanted to eat with him, we invited him to lunch. I now had a lunchtime mission: find a way to draw Bob into the training.

During lunch I asked him, "What do you do at work that you enjoy? What energizes you?"

"Nothing."

Thirty seconds into lunch, and I'm dead in the water. So, I try again.

"So, Bob, what do you do after work that plays to your strengths?"

"Nothing."

Jim and I could see Bob was in real pain.

I tried once more. "Bob, how long has this been going on?"

"Twenty-five years."

"What's the problem?"

"I hate my work, and I hate the people I work with."

Wow. No holding back from Bob on that one. He was blunt and negative, but his response was honest and authentic. I wanted to help him.

"Well, Bob, play this out for me over the next five years. How is this going to affect you, your health, your family?"

Bob dropped his head and slowly shook it back and forth. "I don't know."

Very little changed for Bob during that first day, even as the rest of the team enjoyed discovering their strengths, talents, and learning about their co-workers. In fact, little changed for Bob during all four days.

Bob's Resistance to Change

After the group left, despite some mixed emotions, I couldn't shake Bob from my mind. Clearly, Bob was not engaged in his work and whatever he was doing for his company was draining him to the point of being empty. Obviously, a number of other factors might have been at play outside of work, but like most of us, Bob spent a massive chunk of his waking hours engaged in work. I had a vision of Bob's likely future, even if he wasn't ready to verbalize it. There are real, tangible impacts that result from being misaligned with our purpose and our true abilities.

When our Genius Spark is obscured, the consequence is a tendency to engage in negative and deficit-based self-talk.

If you are constantly engaged in tasks and activities that lie outside of your most natural abilities, it will negatively impact the way you talk to yourself, even if you are technically competent at your job. The subconscious thoughts behind this self-talk are feelings like:

- *"I feel like I'm leaving something on the table. I could be doing more."*
- *"I'm not even that good at this, and I probably never will be."*
- *"If this is as good as I'm going to feel, what's the point of trying much harder?"*

Even in moments of relative optimism, when we feel some sense of what that "more" might look like in our lives, we can still be left with the nagging sensation that something is out of balance, misaligned. In times of stress or anxiety, we can resort back to negative self-talk that might feel normal in the moment, but which is ultimately toxic to our ability to grow and thrive.

The stories we tell ourselves about ourselves can lead to inescapable downward spirals inside our own heads. However, research suggests that negative self-talk often "doesn't have a measurable impact on performance."[8] Counterintuitive as it might seem, you could continue to perform adequately or even impressively at a task that drains you while appearing to the outside world to be another competent and capable employee. In the short term, your capacity to "complete the task" might mitigate some of the misery you experience while doing it, but that isn't sustainable and won't result in long-term satisfaction.

---

8. Tod D, Hardy J, Oliver E. "Effects of self-talk: a systematic review," *J Sport Exerc Psychol.* 2011 Oct;33(5):666-87.

Over time, negative internal narratives lead us to produce lower-quality outputs, both personally and professionally. Before long, we ask ourselves why we should put in much effort if this is about as good as it gets.

Increased levels of chronic and toxic stress lead to measurably worse health outcomes.

People who are "just getting by" and finding themselves consistently engaged in negative self-talk tend to experience higher levels of chronic stress, anxiety, and dissatisfaction. In fact, "83% of US workers suffer from work-related stress, with 25% saying their job is the number one stressor in their lives."[9] The measurable health impacts of this stress are alarming.

In the short-term, chronic stress can lead to various symptoms such as headaches, fatigue, difficulty sleeping, and a weakened immune system. It can also exacerbate health conditions including heart disease, diabetes, and asthma. According to the American Psychological Association, around three-quarters of adults (76 percent) said they have experienced health impacts due to stress in the prior month, including headache (38 percent), fatigue (35 percent), feeling nervous or anxious (34 percent), and/or feeling depressed or sad (33 percent).[10] Furthermore, according to Occupational Health and Safety news and the National Council on Compensation Insurance, up to 90 percent of all visits to primary care physicians are for stress-related complaints. Long-term exposure to chronic stress can also lead to serious health problems such as high blood pressure, heart disease, obesity, and diabetes, and can contribute to developing mental health disorders, such as depression and anxiety.[11]

---

9. "Workplace Stress," *The American Institute of Stress*, February 15, 2023, bit.ly/3NSsbim.

10. "Stress in America 2022." n.d. Https://Www.Apa.Org. https://www.apa.org/news/press/releases/stress/2022/concerned-future-inflation.

11. Salleh, Mohd Razali. "Life event, stress and illness." *The Malaysian journal of medical sciences : MJMS* vol. 15,4 (2008): 9-18.

I don't mean to suggest that misalignment of your purpose is the *only* cause of personal stress and dissatisfaction. There are a multitude of factors that can contribute to a negative, stress-inducing work environment, including poor management, low wages, and unrealistic output expectations. However, I believe it is reasonable to suggest that if our work tasks were more closely aligned with our own capacity and purpose, our daily experiences would include higher levels of fulfillment and satisfaction. In fact, I've seen it happen. Bob's story is just one of many examples.

Rethinking the Pyramid: Placing Self-Actualization at the Center of Human Needs

In Abraham Maslow's Hierarchy of Needs, the eponymous pyramid suggests our fundamental pursuits as humans begin with physiological needs, like food and shelter, and then continue through belonging, community, and self-esteem before arriving at self-actualization. Maslow contended that this hierarchy explained human behavior and motivations.

Imagine a situation where your average worker has nominally acquired each of the needs below the tip of the pyramid. They have a place to live, make enough money to put food on the table, are engaged in a stable, non-abusive relationship with a generally supportive partner, and even have the time to spend in cognitive or intellectual pursuits they find engaging. They should be ready to burst through to the top level of the pyramid, right?

Well, no. Looking at Maslow's hierarchy, we often draw a false equivalency. If I am REALLY GOOD at all the other levels of the pyramid, then I will naturally have access to the final level: self-actualization. Organizations and systems theorists call this way of thinking "sub-optimization," where one attempts to improve a whole system by optimizing each of its constituent parts.

Maslow's Hierarchy
as traditionally pictured

Transcendence

Self Actualization

Self Esteem

Love/Belonging

Safety Needs

Physiological

Unsurprisingly, it doesn't often work like that. Most systems, including us as human beings, are MORE than the sum of their parts. If we think of "self-actualization" as the realization or fulfillment of one's talents and potentialities, we could conclude that it's possible to achieve or reach each of the subordinate levels of the pyramid and still be no closer to attaining the top.

However, Maslow's hierarchy is a bit misleading. Yes, self-actualization deserves a prime spot within any analysis of the relationships inherent between various human pursuits. In fact, that's what this whole book is about. However, rather than place self-actualization as the highest tier of a pyramid, positioning it as the ultimate achievement, it is more appropriate to place it at the center of a nucleus, surrounded by layer upon layer of other human needs.

The truth is that *all* of our needs can be more fully experienced and realized if we seek them while holding our vision of self-actualization firmly in our minds. If we can consistently and confidently define and express our vision of *who* we are at our best, that reassurance will radiate outward, positively impacting every level of our human needs.

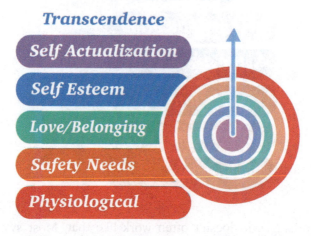

Finding Your Genius Spark:
Language, Insight, Energy, and Repetition

Life looks much different when the work we do, the choices we make, and the relationships we build all flow out of our natural talents, curiosities, and passions. Imagine waking up in the morning, lying in bed and thinking about the day ahead. Unlike the dread most of us have felt in that position, knowing we're about to spend nine hours drained and dissatisfied, you feel eager to get to work, because you know throughout the day you'll be drawing upon your inherent talents and skills as you navigate the challenges and tasks to come. Your best self is needed and valued in the settings where you'll find yourself throughout the day. It's not hard to see that when we center how we spend our lives around our inherent talents, it positively affects everything else: our physiology, our relationships, our sense of belonging, our self-esteem.

Steve Jobs, the billionaire genius behind Apple Computers, had a basic policy for how he approached his days: "For the past

33 years, I have looked in the mirror every morning and asked my-self: 'If today were the last day of my life, would I want to do what I am about to do today?' And whenever the answer has been 'No' for too many days in a row, I know I need to change something."

The Power of Alignment:
Unveiling Bob's True Talents

Three months after I met Bob during the training, I returned to lead a second workshop with the company. This time I was teaching those same managers how to coach their direct reports. When I entered the room, I ran into Bob, and he was smiling. No slouch. No folded arms. No caustic comments. I was shocked. On the second day of the training, Bob stood and told the room, "I love my job and love you all." I wasn't expecting anything like this. The formerly depressed, surly Bob touched the emotions of the entire room.

I found Bob's boss, Roy, at the break. "What happened to Bob?" I asked.

Roy told me Bob asked if they could have dinner during the initial training three months ago. During the dinner, Bob was able to tell Roy why he was miserable. More than that, Bob asked for help.

Roy learned why Bob was so angry, frustrated, and withdrawn. His top core talents included four thinking/processing strengths traits and one that focused on getting things done. His top five talents were internal, related to thinking and doing. But Bob's job focused on external issues: people, conflict, and ongoing crises. He had to deal with contentious union reps and people who often felt little accountability for their performance. So, Bob's job required external strengths/talents, but Bob had no external talents.

Imagine coming to work every day for 25 years drained, inef-fective, unequipped, and clueless about the dynamics of your job. Bob remained depleted, angry, acting out, and going through the motions with no insight for tapping into his core talents

In the three months between our meetings, Roy basically saved Bob's life by revitalizing his career. He reassigned him to research and development on a critical future initiative for the organization. The new role tapped into three of Bob's top talents: deep thinking, new learning, and futuristic research. After 60 days in this new role, Bob became a new person.

From Misery to Fulfillment:
Bob's Journey of Rediscovery

Bob never knew he was wired to work in a particular way. He thought everyone felt the way he did about work. Bob did not realize he had talents that could be identified and intentionally used. He was like most of us: vaguely aware of what we're good at, but unaware of how clarity about our talents can make a big difference in our lives—at work and home.

Prior to the training, Bob had no skills to deal with any work situation that went against his grain. He had no language, insight, or strategy to help him change his circumstances. Sadly, most managers don't have the framework that his boss, Roy, had learned to leverage. Roy had gained insight into dealing with Bob and others like him. As a result, Roy and Bob could talk about their mutual problem in a shared, productive, and life-changing way. Incredibly, neither Bob nor Roy were "experts." All they needed was a little insight into Bob's wiring and a shared vocabulary to talk about it. Bob's dramatic story started with a small light switch turning on: "Aha! I have natural talents, and they can help me succeed and enjoy life."

Eighty percent of our time is spent doing tasks outside our natural talents—tasks others can do better and enjoy more. The good news is in the following chapters, you will learn how you can live differently, too.

Uncomplicating Self-Improvement:
Simple Shifts for Radical Results

Anecdotes like Bob's shouldn't be uncommon. These stories of simple shifts making a radical difference should be the rule, but we've made "self-improvement" so much more complicated than it needs to be.

The self-improvement industry is expected to represent a 67

billion dollar chunk of the global economy by 2030. Considering what we've already learned about the current state of workplace wellbeing, it shouldn't surprise us that the market has responded with all kinds of products, courses, systems, and speakers all claiming to have THE answers to our nagging suspicions that we could be *more* than we are right now. You know the products and the marketing slogans:

"Come take our course on 'BEING A BETTER YOU.' For three easy payments of $299.99 you'll get access to our EXTENSIVE library of close to FOUR HUNDRED LESSONS and almost TWO million hours of motivational videos. Follow our easy 48-step process and you too can be the best you."

The self-improvement industry makes several faulty assumptions that have perpetuated both explosive growth and less-than-optimal results.

- They tell us that increased knowledge inevitably leads to increased success, when in reality there is no substitute for repeated experience.
- They tell us that we must "identify our *why*" before leading us to clearly define *who* we are and *what* we are most clearly capable of.
- They suggest that if we don't succeed in their programs, we should take responsibility for the failure and then prompt us to purchase more products to remedy our challenge in order to achieve our desired success.
- And perhaps most egregious of all, they consistently tell us that progress will be easy but complicated (that is, they rely on exhaustive frameworks, limitless exercises, and session after session after session of work for their participants).

The secret is that it's not complicated. It's simple, but it won't be easy. The rediscovery and tending of our Genius Spark requires four things: Language, Insight, Energy, and Repetition. I won't claim to have all of the answers, but I believe I've developed some key tools to support you in your pursuit of who you actually are, and what you're actually capable of. Over the next three chapters you will:

- Develop clear **language** that describes your vision of yourself at your best.
- Seek **insights** into your own behaviors and motivations by implementing a simple practice of consideration and reflection
- Make choices and set goals tailored to leverage your strengths, reigniting your **energy** and allowing you to experience life with significantly less drain.

By shifting our personal practice and focus to the essential question of what makes each of us uniquely US, we can move closer to a state where we can make magic on purpose, and be invigorated, rather than drained, during our daily lives.

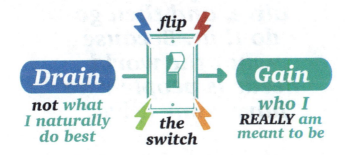

As we conclude this chapter, we see the power and importance of aligning our talents and passions with our work. Bob's transformation reminds us that finding fulfillment requires a deep understanding of our true selves. While Abraham Maslow's Hierarchy of Needs offers valuable insights, we must also challenge its limitations. Instead of placing self-actualization at the pinnacle, we recognize it as the nucleus surrounded by layers of other human needs. By consistently defining and expressing our vision of who we are at our best, we can positively impact every level of our human needs. Building upon this understanding, Chapter Four will delve into the critical role of language in uncovering and nurturing our Genius Spark. Through the process of creating our Genius Portrait, we will clear away the debris of self-doubt and uncertainty, enabling us to move closer to our flow state and unlock our full potential.

"Do not ask yourself what the world needs. Ask yourself what makes you come alive, and then go do that. Because what the world needs is people who have come alive."

- Howard Thurman

Key Lessons for Chapter Three: Breaking the Cycle

1. **Alignment for Fulfillment:** Bob's resistance to change and disengagement from work highlighted the importance of aligning one's natural talents and passions with their job.
2. **Consequences of Misalignment:** Misalignment with one's purpose and natural abilities can lead to chronic stress, dissatisfaction, and negative self-talk.
3. **Maslow's Hierarchy Reconsidered:** Abraham Maslow's Hierarchy of Needs, while valuable, can be misleading when it comes to achieving self-actualization.
4. **Holistic Approach to Fulfillment:** Placing self-actualization at the center of a nucleus, surrounded by other human needs, allows for a more holistic approach to personal fulfillment.
5. **Elements of Rediscovery:** Language, insight, energy, and repetition are the key elements in rediscovering and tending to one's Genius Spark.
6. **Simplicity in Personal Growth:** The self-improvement industry often overcomplicates the process of personal development, leading to less-than-optimal results.
7. **Radical Transformations through Simplicity:** Simple shifts and focusing on one's unique talents and potentialities can lead to radical transformations in both career and life.
8. **Expressing the Best Self:** By consistently defining and expressing one's vision of their best self, all human needs can be more fully experienced and realized.

Chapter 4

Defining Your Genius

It's unbelievable how much you don't know about the game you've been playing all your life.

—Billy Beane

When the Obvious is Hidden: Unveiling Hidden Potential

Lilly, a teacher and a gifted person, called me to ask for career advice. As a child, she loved art and was quite talented. However, during high school, two dream stealers entered Lilly's world. Her parents urged her to keep art as a hobby and go into teaching. The other villain was, ironically, the art teacher. One of Lilly's dragons was her combination of ADHD and dyslexia. One day the teacher assigned the art class to go outside and quickly sketch a series of objects. Lilly got so absorbed in a single leaf that she spent the whole time creating a beautiful drawing. The teacher responded by threatening to fail her unless she handed over a completed portfolio of the assigned work. She would be the judge of what could count as art, and who could count as an artist. The choice left Lilly heartbroken, and it remains a fresh wound more than thirty years later.

Lilly works with students on the autism spectrum. She told me she spends her days encouraging students to explore their interests. She watched them carefully, identified and celebrated what made them unique, and then made sure that other people, including their parents and peers, got to see that beautiful uniqueness. These 'typical days' sounded to me a lot like an artist seeking and uplifting things that they thought the world deserved to see. She was very much trying to connect with that lost sense of creativity, but I wasn't sure she could see it. So I asked her to reflect on her strengths and interests, hoping to discover keys to her lost genius.

"Lilly," I asked, "do you enjoy what you're doing?"

"I love my kids and the progress I see," she responded.

"Does anyone else get the kind of results you do?"

"Not even close; I'm willing to think outside the box and treat each child individually like I wished I'd been treated. The school isn't set up to do that."

I thought to myself. *She's there, it's right in front of her, but her wounds won't let her see it.*

"Lilly," I followed up, "I'm a little confused. You're so animated and happy when you talk about your kids and your work with them. But I can't square that with how sad you look and sound when you talk about teaching."

Reluctantly, almost wistfully, she shared an insight. "I recently attended an organization of volunteer artists and felt like I found my tribe. It reminded me of what I missed out on not pursuing art."

And that was it. That disconnect was the problem, and it was also the key to reigniting her Genius Spark.

"You know, of course," I told her, "being an artist is not just painting. It's part of it, but not all its potential. I can see you're an artist; it's who you are. Now you have a clear portrait of the type of artist, no matter where you are or what you're doing. I've never heard a teacher describe what she does in such artistic language. Your classroom feels like a canvas, and your kids your color palette. And what's notable is you treat each one as uniquely gifted and special because that comes so naturally. I think you're so close but still locked out because of what you feel was stolen by your teacher and the giving into your parents' expectations. Your journey is to slay that dragon and let go. Embrace the artist you are. If you do, your story will change, and you'll be able to unlock the positive energy that comes with living into your strengths."

After our conversation, I sent Lilly a link to take one of the assessments we use. With a little bit of time and self-reflection, and through the help of our free web app, she created the following description of her genius traits:

I am the go-to catalyst when someone is stuck. I can see the hidden strengths and beauty in others and help them realize their potential. I practice the Golden Rule and treat people how I want to be treated. I

am naturally curious and love to explore and talk about new things. I understand and accept that things in life happen for a reason, even if they are difficult.

That brief but encompassing paragraph is what I call Lilly's Genius Portrait. When Lilly was able to put specific language to her natural abilities, she was better able to understand how to harness those talents and use them to accomplish her goals and live a more satisfying life. Language consolidates our understanding of our genius potential. By composing our Genius Portrait, we lay the foundation for accessing our Genius Spark. In our formula **Language + Insight + Energy = Magic**, the first step is finding the words that describe our true self.

Word Craft: Harnessing the Language of Genius

Language is one of the primary mechanisms by which humans construct meaning and create order within their lives. The specific words we choose to use, whether verbally or in written form, are indicators that can reveal the unique way we view the world. Just as cultural nuances and regional dialects exist for a spoken language, so too do we see individual peculiarities within an individual person's speech pattern. Many times, those unique elements within someone's manner of speaking can offer us insight into how their brain is wired, and which of their natural traits and talents they most readily lean into.

Since our speech is already impacted directly by our inherent qualities, language makes sense as a starting place for making magic on purpose. In order to effectively utilize the set of habits, skills, and mindsets an individual is most likely to utilize to successfully pursue a goal or outcome, we must develop language and descriptions that succinctly and confidently define, describe, and communicate those qualities. Naming them is the only way that an individual will be able to identify, express, and develop fluency with their unique capacity for contribution.

Many of us, like Lilly, have natural talents that are easily identified but, like Bob from chapter three, they are not aligned with the task at hand, whether personal or professional. We are often stuck in what I call the "drain zone," and our talents are misaligned with the actions we take at work and in our relationships. In that zone, the demands and pressures we face literally drain our energy rather than enabling us to use that energy to thrive. The first and most important step toward meaningful, satisfying change is to *develop clear, understandable language that describes us at our best.* This process is part ecological conservation and part archaeology. We're going to dredge waterways that are full of silt, clearing away the debris of self-doubt and general uncertainty. We will shore up the banks and reinforce the levees so we can clearly see what we look and feel like when we are thriving. We will identify moments that changed our course and moments that solidified it. Once we're able to accurately and confidently describe what we look like at our best, we will be able to consistently move toward that state in our daily lives.

You may not have to look far if you're curious and searching. The start of your adventure may be in your own backyard. In fact, it usually is. Doesn't the hero in all the great stories typically return to the place they started? They're not the same person, but instead of abandoning the past, they bring to it the power and vitality of those around them. Joseph Campbell says, "We're not on our journey to save the world but to save ourselves. But in doing that, you save the world. The influence of a vital person vitalizes."[12] The opportunity to unleash your genius potential is thrilling, but the stakes are high. The world, at least the world around you, depends on you reclaiming and nurturing your full potential.

12. Campbell, Joseph, and Diane K. Osbon. 1991. *A Joseph Campbell Companion: Reflections on the Art of Living.* http://ci.nii.ac.jp/ncid/BA49906130.

Crafting Your Genius Portrait: Illuminating Your True Self

When Michelangelo was asked about his masterpiece statue of the Biblical figure David, he was reported to have said, "I created a vision of David in my mind and simply carved away everything that was not David." How do we find the hidden masterpiece within us, and how can the Genius Spark help us to find our own David? Let's pop the hood and take a look at how the process works.

Like Lilly, you can use summaries from any assessment and distill them into a clear, unique Genius Portrait. The CliftonStrengths®, for example, identifies and ranks 34 talent themes, focusing on an individual's top five. Reading your report is the starting point to see why some things come naturally and enjoyably and others don't. Hidden inside these reports is an inspiring portrait of your ideal self. The process described in this book will help you find it.

Many assessment reports assemble a series of pre-written paragraphs with general descriptions of a person's different traits. When you read through your results, it's common to read some sentences that connect immediately and others that don't quite fit. After leafing through thousands of reports with clients and scanning pages of boilerplate text, I always find a handful of sentences that resonate and capture what fully energizes and motivates them. However, I haven't found a system that provides a process to chip away and find that handful of essential traits, the Genius Spark.

I will share my process so you can find your version of David inside these reports—you can also use the free Genius Spark web app to make it even easier. Once you have chipped away and released that beautiful image of your ideal self, you can step back and start to appreciate and see other hidden features. After 20 years of encouraging clients to take 15 minutes to personalize their reports, I've learned that fewer than 1 percent actually do it. But creating a personalized portrait lays the foundation for igniting your Genius Spark. Just knowing about your strongest traits isn't enough. The pandemic exposed that mistake. Once the work treadmill stopped, many of my clients experienced a profound loss of identity and purpose. Helping them work through their challenges and articulating their unique traits became the catalyst behind the Genius Spark. The LANGUAGE we use to talk to and about ourselves matters immensely. The stories we construct about what we are and are not good at end up playing out as self-fulfilling prophecies. Thus, the adoption of this Genius Portrait is our first step on the path toward making magic on purpose.

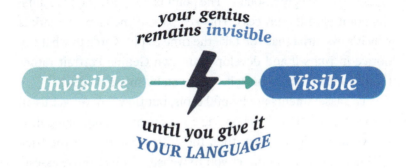

Painting a Vivid Picture: Describing Your Unique Brilliance

There are three steps to crafting a Genius Portrait. First, we must identify and describe our natural talents and traits. Second, we must categorize those qualities to give us a sense of how people built like us generally approach the world around them. Though we are each originals, we can learn by looking at others who share similarities in their strengths and tendencies. Finally, we'll compose a simple paragraph that uses this information to paint a picture of what we look like at our best.

There are many resources and assessments to tell us who we are and help us put words to the genius traits we possess, Myers Briggs, DISC, the Enneagram, and CliftonStrengths®, to name a few. All of these assessments offer unique insights, and none are perfect. Most people who take a personality test will view their results with a mixture of insight and skepticism. Pieces of your results are likely to describe you to a T and make you say, "wow, that is TOTALLY me." Other elements can be more puzzling and feel like they miss the mark. That is okay.

You're unlikely ever to have a 100 percent accurate representation of yourself handed to you on a piece of paper with bar graphs and personality-type descriptions. Still, it's not about the description being perfect: It's about the description capturing elements that deeply resonate. The point is not perfect end results; the point is in the process. This key part of the Genius Spark is why it's essential that you take the time to put words to what *you* notice in *yourself* and develop your own Genius Portrait rather than adopt a description spit out at you by an assessment.

The assessments are helpful tools, but they'll never get us all the way there. Start by choosing an assessment and taking it. If you've never done a test, then there are resources in the back of this book that will direct you to websites where those assessments are available. They are not our final destination but a starting place. I created the Genius Spark app to help the majority of people who need a simple way to get started. Once you begin you'll create a unique compelling portrait of what you look like at your best in as little as 15 minutes.

Step 1: Discovering Your Genius Traits: The Foundation of Genius

First, we must look at the results of your personality assessment. If you've taken an assessment like the CliftonStrengths®, your results are conveniently listed as 'Strengths' already. If you've used something like the Myers Briggs, DISC or the Enneagram, your results are slightly different. Regardless of the report, you can pull out what you need. As you read through your report or reports, simply *highlight the sentences* that best capture those your strongest and best traits.

Look at your results and jot down sentences and phrases that resonate with you. What you're looking for is any moments of clarity where what's written on the page is PRETTY DARN CLOSE to describing how you actually experience the world around you. When that happens, go ahead and write it down.

IMPORTANT NOTE: many of these assessments mix what they define as your weaknesses with your strengths. We will discuss the idea of weaknesses later. For now, form your sentences in a **positive, declarative manner.** My recommendation is to make a bulleted list of about 10 characteristics. Once you have come up with the statements that resonate with you, read them over a few times, maybe even try saying them out loud. How does it feel? Do those words represent you? Do you feel like there's something more that's not expressed, even if the statements feel true of you? If that's the case, you're right where you should be to move on to Step 2.

Step 2: Embracing your Archetype: Patterns and Interactions

Several assessments use a four-quadrant model to group traits into common categories. Examples include the CliftonStrengths®, DISC, Whole Brain® Thinking Model, The Four Temperaments, Myers Briggs, and Competing Values®. These four-quadrant models provide a lens that identifies concentrations of traits and patterns.

For the Genius Spark, I designed the Ring System, which provides a similar four-zone visual model but differs by representing the zones along a circle or ring to better designate concentrated zones and archetypal patterns. This visualization helps you identify your zones, their concentrations, and the different combinations. There are fifteen combinations I have distilled into character archetypes. In the appendix of this book, you will find a description of each Ring archetype, and you can use them as a frame of reference. It helps to know your genius traits and how they relate to interplay with one another. That's what the Ring System illustrates.

In the Ring System, the Genius Spark groups your assessment results into four colored zones—blue: relating traits; green: thinking traits; orange: acting traits; and red: motivating traits—to simplify and present a tailored description of what you look like at your best. The Ring System organizes the traits you uncovered in your assessment like a deck of cards. When you see someone's Ring, you grasp an immediate window into their personality, intuitive capabilities, and sources of energy. Moving from the rings to the different combinations of strengths provides a wide range of understanding, like moving from a telescopic view to a microscopic one.

To identify WHICH of the four zones is most dominant for you, you will look at the list you made in Step 1. Label each of the items on your list with the name of one of the zones: Acting, Thinking, Motivating, or Relating. This doesn't have to be perfect. Your archetype description is the resource we will use to start crafting your Genius Portrait.

The Four Zones

Interpersonal talents are **blue** and grouped in the **Relating zone.** People with relating traits absorb emotional energy, operate like emotional thermometers, and quickly "read" non-verbal cues. The traits range from sensing to bridging to bonding.

The **green** cognitive talents are in the **Thinking zone**, ranging from input to processing and reaching decisions. People with those traits feel energized when they can retreat into their heads.

Initiating talents (**orange**) that start, sustain, and complete a task are in the **Acting zone**. I like to call these the "get-er-done" traits.

Talents that help people prompt others to action are **red** and are in the **Motivating zone**. Those people operate like emotional thermostats and instinctively know how to increase energy and enthusiasm or accomplish a task or a mission.

Finding Your Zones

There are 15 combinations of zones, or rings, that give us a starting point. Your core traits, when activated, release energy and function instinctively in real-time, like a first language. The rings reveal a dominant energy field and natural fluency when your strengths are grouped by their zones. You can find a description of each ring in the addendum.

Step 3: Crafting and Drafting Your Genius Portrait

Now, it's time to craft a Genius Portrait. This 5–6 sentence paragraph is written in a declarative tone to paint a picture of what you look like at your best. It's a picture of when you are leaning most heavily into your core talents. There is no "right way" to craft your Genius Portrait—each is individual and unique—but I will give you some helpful guidelines.

1. This is not a novel: Your paragraph should be just that, a paragraph, a few sentences in length.

2. Keep the essentials: You have a lot of input, from the results of your personality assessment to your archetype description. Be reasonable about what makes it into your paragraph, and only keep the descriptors you feel most strongly about.

By taking a large number of personal descriptors and distilling them into an essential set of *personally chosen* phrases, we can begin to see an image of what someone looks like when their Genius

Spark is on full display. It can be mesmerizing to watch someone at work in their genius flow.

Cracking the Code: Understanding the Ring System and Color Classifications

The first step toward mastery is to understand how to use the color classifications in my Ring System. Most assessments group results into a color system, commonly falling into four categories. The Genius Spark identifies Relating traits with blue, Motivating with red, Acting with orange, and Thinking with green. The colors function like a deck of cards and allow you to immediately recognize dominant zones, natural intuition, sources of energy, and genius patterns.

Think of each zone like a language and each trait like a dialect. The more traits you have in a zone makes you more fluent and instinctive. For example, someone with three Relating traits reads non-verbal cues incredibly well, in real time. Those who have a dominant Motivating zone read individual and group energy and engagement. These two right brain functions understand relational tones, tempos, and rhythms.

Those with dominant Thinking zones take inputs distill thoughts into ideas, facts, logic, patterns, connections and decisions sometimes quickly and sometimes after deep reflection. Those with dominant Acting zones are naturally driven to start, sustain and complete something. They get things done. You don't have to be an expert about individual traits. You can look at their color ring and immediately see similarities and differences. That is a great place to start.

I designed the Genius Portrait to reinforce a vivid word picture of what you look like at your best. This is not a one-and-done exercise. The portrait is a reinforcement and simulation tool to revive your buried genius traits. This tool provides a starting point. I'll share a few examples of how some clients started their portraits, then watched them grow. As you read these samples, think about how you might describe yourself in similar ways, but tailored to you. Focus on specific word choices, especially strong verbs and descriptive words.

Identifying Dominant Zones—Ana's Example

Ana was a born project planner. All she needed to know was the tools she had available and the desired end goal—that, and the ice cold Diet Coke she'd crack open before each team meeting. From there she could develop timelines, identify key goalposts, and synthesize huge amounts of information to formulate a clear and logical plan of attack. Ana's neural pathways were built ideally for things like analytical thinking, strategic planning, and pattern identification. Using this set of skills felt to Ana like floating swiftly down the Mississippi on a sturdy barge. Surrounded by timelines and spreadsheets, she could see *so clearly* a path through the confusion to success and completion. After taking an assessment and identifying key traits and talents, these are the zones that Ana identified from her list of qualities.

What Resonated with Me

1. *I enjoy coaching and developing others* (Motivating)
2. *I like to plan ahead* (Thinking)
3. *I tend to be able to get others moving forward relatively quickly* (Motivating)
4. *I am the go-to person to get something started* (Acting)
5. *I am most energized when I feel like I'm making progress on something I care about* (Acting)
6. *I tend to begin with a goal and work my way backward to a plan* (Thinking)
7. *I have a strong desire to GET GOING* (Acting)
8. *I quickly identify patterns and themes* (Thinking)

9. *When my thoughts settle, I'm ready to act* (*Thinking/
   Acting*)
10. *I can keep going as long as I feel like there is momentum*
    (*Acting*)

By reviewing Ana's traits and how they align with the various rings, we can identify tendencies that enable her to thrive. For example, Ana has core talents in the Acting, Thinking, and Motivating zones. Looking at the ring archetypes, we would classify her as a 'Juggernaut.' Here is a sample from the 'Juggernaut' archetype description:

Juggernauts are typically strong, energetic, internally driven people who motivate people to achieve. They are intelligent in the areas of their traits and dynamic where they concentrate. Rarely do others bump them off course. Juggernauts are sometimes loners who move forward despite road hazards.

After taking an assessment, identifying her rings, and considering all of the descriptors in front of her, here's the Genius Portrait that Ana wrote.

"I like to start with the end in mind and work my way backward. I love to develop and mentor others, especially in subjects where I feel confident. When I get the feel and flavor of a direction or goal, I want to spin talk into action and ideas into intentionality. I can synthesize large amounts of complex information into essential elements and communicate them effectively. I instinctively know what it will take to get something done and can support the people who will make it happen."

> *"The single most important factor in creative achievement is your ability to get back the native, untutored genius we all have in childhood."*

> *- George Land*

The Genius Language: Harnessing the Power of Self-Talk

The LANGUAGE we use to talk to and about ourselves matters immensely, and Ana's Genius Portrait provides a succinct reminder of her key qualities, traits, and talents that allow her to be her best. The stories we construct about what we are and are not good at end up playing out as self-fulfilling prophecies, and the adoption of the Genius Portrait is our first step on the path toward making magic on purpose. As Dale Carnegie once wrote in his bestselling book *How to Win Friends and Influence People*, "What the mind can conceive and believe, the mind can achieve."

Crafting a Genius Portrait is an important exercise in mindfulness and affirmation, for putting words to our general ideas of how we function and excel is a key step in reinforcing those core talents and reminding ourselves of our inner genius. Like any piece of writing, your Genius Portrait may take some crafting and editing. Keep working at it until you are proud of its authenticity and you feel inspired by reading it. That positivity will increase the likelihood you use it regularly to remind yourself of your Genius Spark.

Here are some additional examples of Genius Portraits with brief descriptions of the individual behind the magic.

Genius Portrait #1:
Unleashing the Project Manager's Brilliance

This person is a project manager for a $1 billion hospital bed tower project. He identified his core talents as: Navigation - Creativity - Persuasiveness - Driver - Fearlessness

I make split-second decisions by processing and considering all alternatives and discarding fruitless/inferior options. I have an active and vivid imagination that generates energy and fosters a quirky sense of humor. I often utilize simple but powerful stories and metaphors to bring clarity to complex issues and situations. To a fault, I continually create a physical or virtual list of tasks to be completed. I am energized by rapidly creating momentum and turning ideas into immediate action.

Genius Portrait #2:
Empowering Connections as an HR Director

The person is a human resources director for a software company. She sees her core talents as: Cheerfulness - Persuasiveness - Genuineness - Fixer - Empathy

I move people into a better space, place, and mind by appreciating who they are and what they do. Words are my currency for building bridges and strengthening relationships. I have a fine-tuned sense of if someone is genuine or not and, therefore, will keep people at bay until they reach my threshold of trust. I love to be a part of the solution because it brings things back to life. I can sense what is not being said and give it expression, which draws people in and allows them to feel heard.

Genius Portrait #3:
Energizing as a Social Media Consultant

This person is a social media consultant who identifies her core talents as: Scholarship - Curiosity - Accomplishment - Navigation - Persistence

I remember details that don't seem important to others, which prove useful later. My mind allows me to go from topic to topic. I will read and then listen to podcasts. I feel incredibly energized when I cross off to-dos and am ready to do more and more! Usually, I can visualize the end of a story before it is finished, which helps me move toward that and see the next steps. When I hit obstacles, I can overcome and persevere to get the job done.

Genius Portrait #4:
Leading with Confidence in Construction

This person is a construction project executive for a hospital system. His core talents are identified as: Accomplishment—Curiosity—Confidence—Scholarship—Vigilant

I don't like to sit around; I'll always find something to do. Vacations are jam-packed—no days lounging on the beach for me! I can ramp up quickly on a topic or a project—I get "it" pretty quick. When I come to a decision or direction, I am almost immoveable with confidence and conviction. I can think through complex issues and consider the implications of different choices. I can see the unintended consequences that others can't, four to five steps ahead, and sometimes beyond.

Genius Portrait #5:
Progress and Expansion of a Marketing Director

This last example illustrates what progress can look like over time. This client started with our template, expanded it to include her top 10 strengths, and added the Virtues in Action Character Strengths Survey results.[13] She is a marketing director for a large engineering firm. Her core talents are: Visionary - Cheerfulness - Navigation - Charm - Fearlessness - Persuasiveness - Optimization - Hospitality - Excellence - Principled

---

13. "The VIA Character Strengths Survey," *VIA Institute On Character*, www.viacharacter.org/character-strengths.

I live every breath in awareness of God and the beauty of creation. I'm fueled by a deep belief that something in each human is holy and of infinite value. I know I can be part of the recovery of the world through small acts of kindness, forgiveness, creativity, and love. I'm strong and intrinsically motivated. I'm fascinated by being part of what is coming and am fulfilled by positive forward motion. When I give my attention to something, I rarely get pulled off course. I focus on worthy things with split-second processing. I consider unexpected alternatives and discard fruitless options. I get great joy from working with organizations and individuals to encourage and inspire them toward a better future. I identify commonalities between people, build rapport, then mobilize them to connect. I rapidly create momentum by turning ideas into immediate action. I have clarity and conviction and share a genuine joy in life. I love the dynamics of working in a well-aligned team.

From Core Talents to Flow—Unleashing the Power

In the next chapter I'll introduce the concept of flow as described by Mihaly Csikszentmihalyi. Flow refers to a state of complete absorption and optimal intrinsic motivation, where individuals are happiest and most productive. By understanding and harnessing our natural talents and traits, we can enter the state of flow and experience the numerous benefits it brings in terms of productivity, well-being, and fulfillment. That section also highlights the importance of deep work, deep love, deep thought, and deep connection in leading a satisfying and meaningful life. It emphasizes the need to focus on our strengths and engage in immersive activities that align with our core talents to experience the profound rewards of flow.

Key Lessons of Chapter Four: Defining Your Genius

1. **Overcoming Limiting Beliefs:** Sometimes our true genius is right in front of us, but wounds and limiting beliefs can prevent us from seeing it clearly.

2. **Creating a Vivid Self-Image:** Creating a concise paragraph that describes what we look like at our best helps to paint a vivid picture of our strengths and core talents.

3. **The Power of Words:** The words we use to describe ourselves and our abilities shape our self-perception and influence our actions and achievements.

4. **Uniqueness of the Genius Portrait:** Each individual's Genius Portrait is unique and should reflect their own strengths, interests, and aspirations.

5. **Genius Portrait as a Tool:** A well-crafted Genius Portrait serves as a reinforcement and simulation tool, helping us revive and develop our buried genius traits.

6. **Impact of Self-Talk:** The language we use to talk to ourselves matters greatly, as our self-perceptions and stories shape our beliefs and actions.

7. **Reinforcing Your Genius Portrait:** Crafting and regularly revisiting your Genius Portrait reinforces your core talents, boosts self-confidence, and helps you make intentional progress toward your goals.

Chapter 5

Visualize, Verbalize, Materialize

"Visualization is daydreaming with a purpose"

—Bo Bennet

A global engineering firm recently bought the company Christine works for. She was head of marketing for a specialty engineering firm of about 40 employees. Her role merged under a centralized marketing department now serving more than 1,500 employees.

The change turned her world upside down. It removed the freedom and creativity she had enjoyed. Her focus shifted from curating the firm's public presence to attending meetings and writing reports. She also found that she was the new kid on the block despite her success, experience, and credentials. In a word, she felt deflated and uncertain about her future.

Like Rachel and Bob and Lilly, Christine has natural talents and genius traits, and she worked hard to use those qualities in pursuing her goals. To that point, she had lived a reasonably successful life, both personally and professionally. But life had thrown her a curveball, and she found herself stuck in the drain zone. When I worked with Christine, she was wrestling with several competing needs.

- "I've got to consider that I am the breadwinner for our family."
- "My office is like family. We've been together for almost 20 years."
- "I hate having to play the corporate game and spend more time managing the dynamics at corporate than doing the work."
- "A lot of my decision depends on how long Jim (the firm's founder) stays. If he stays, I have a base of support to operate from."
- "Is it time for me to do my own thing?"

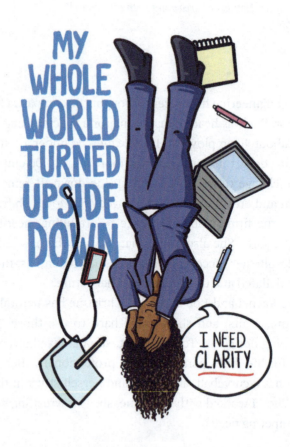

Reconnecting with Your Genius Traits: Meditation and Sketch Journaling

I've known Christine for almost 20 years. Her practice of meditation and sketch journaling helps her look at all the moving parts, find clarity, see the bigger picture, and operate with conviction. When she visited me for a retreat we talked a bit about her challenges, but she spent most of the time walking along the bluff and the creek on our ranch.[14] She sat on the back deck or our guest house scribbling in her journal. Through that reflection and focus on language, we were able to reconnect her to her genius traits and develop a portrait of what it looks like on her best day. Here is what she wrote.

I live every breath in awareness of God and the beauty of creation. I'm fueled by a deep belief that something in each human is holy and of infinite value. I know I can be part of the world's recovery, accomplished through small acts of kindness, forgiveness, creativity, and love. I'm strong, energetic, and intrinsically motivated. I'm fascinated by being part of what is to come and am fulfilled by positive forward motion. When I give attention to something, I stay on course. I find and focus on worthy things with split-second processing. I consider various unanticipated alternatives and discard fruitless options to find novel solutions. I get great joy from working with organizations and individuals to encourage and inspire them toward a better future. I identify commonalities between people, build rapport, mobilize them to connect and turn ideas into action. I bring clarity and conviction and share a genuine joy of life. I love the dynamics of working in a well-aligned team. My best days are when I can elevate something or someone.

---

14. River Rose is an idyllic retreat ranch that offers a sanctuary where weary individuals can rejuvenate their spirits, rekindle their creativity, and forge meaningful bonds with one another.

The Dilemma:
New Role vs. Doing Her Own Thing

When Christine initially read the description and then considered the new challenge in her job, her first reaction was, "I don't think this new role is a good fit." Our conversation fluctuated between her inclination to leave her job and start a consulting firm and her reservations about what she would give up if she left a stable job. She was right about the new reality—it would suck the life out of her. However, there were still many variables in motion with the merger, and she benefited from processing the changes in her company and her understanding of her own best self, operating in sync with her genius traits. With her new clarity, she could better advocate and shape her future.

If she quit her job and went out on her own, the liberation could be empowering. However, after a short honeymoon, the new realities and pressures of going out on her own would build up and might be worse than her initial situation. She could be proverbially jumping out of the frying pan and into a new fire. By creating her Genius Portrait and using her time at the ranch to reconnect with the source of her magic and joy, Christine was able to settle her internal battle of doubt. She clarified who she is at her best and what kind of work allows and supports that. When she returned to work, Christine felt prepared to have an honest and candid heart-to-heart with her old boss, sharing why she had struggled in the new structure and how she could make the biggest contribution. She also asked her boss the big question, "How long are you planning to stay with the firm?"

In the end, a combination of events resulted in a new role opening at her company, one that provided Christine with the creative platform she desired and on a much bigger stage. She called to tell me, both hopeful and anxious. She had to apply and compete for it. You know the ending: She got the position and is thrilled.

Reactions to the Genius Portrait: Giggles, Contemplation, and Ownership

When people read their Genius Portrait for the first time, they have a variety of reactions. They have undergone significant reflection and tailored language to describe themselves at their best, so this is understandable. Some people giggle. They look at this little verbal reflection of themselves, and they're tickled to see it on paper. It can be overwhelming to see some of the best parts of yourself distilled right in front of you. Even more so because it didn't come from a set of clinical, sterile assessment results—it's personal, created by the person who knows you best. Others are quiet. Looking over what they've composed, they're contemplative. I think this is because even then, they are beginning to understand the implications of what they've done, and having captured this snapshot of their best selves, they start to wonder: "What if this was true all the time?"

But all people who complete a Genius Portrait exhibit significant ownership over their paragraph. "This is mine," they realize. "I wrote it, and I *want* to own it and lean into making it work for me." They can already see the next step in this process before it begins. They know instinctively that this is a tool they can use to gain *insight* into how they can make magic on purpose.

In the past 20 years, psychometric tools have become essential to gaining reliable insight into our personalities, natural strengths, potential weaknesses, and performance under pressure. The Positive Psychology movement, coined in 1998, is shifting the focus of managers, counselors, teachers, and parents from what's wrong to building what's strong. Once you develop your Genius Portrait, you are ready to put into practice the same high-performance principles that pilots, professional athletes, and Navy SEALs follow, mental rehearsal and reflection.

From Drain to Flow:
Mastery and Optimal Motivation

Mihaly Csikszentmihalyi's research into happiness led to the theory that people are happiest when they are in complete absorption with everything that is happening in their lives at the moment. People have described it as the moment when they are "firing on all cylinders," times when everything seems in sync, and it all works out. Csikszentmihalyi termed this state "flow," and he described it as "moments of optimal experience." Flow has become a well-known term for describing the state of effortless operation, whether at work or absorbed in an activity. Athletes often refer to it as being "in the zone." Another way to describe flow is a state of "optimal intrinsic motivation."[15]

Csikszentmihalyi's model describes a continuum of psychological states from boredom, relaxation, control, flow, arousal, anxiety, worry, and apathy. If mapped on an X/Y axis, one range registers challenge, and the other registers skill level. The Goldilocks zone for deep absorption activates our strengths; not too easy or too hard, but just right. That just-right zone is about four percent beyond our skill level.

When you drop into a flow state, you find many productivity, health, and well-being benefits.[16] There are also grave concerns about living in a world where distractions and social media shred our attention. Author and Georgetown computer science professor Cal Newport contrasts these two states as deep and shallow work.[17] In my previous book, *The Healthy Workplace Nudge*, I discuss how these distractions bring significant work stress and a lack of

---

15. Mihaly Csikszentmihalyi, *Flow: The Psychology of Optimal Experience* (New York: Harper and Row, 2009).

16. "The Benefits of Flow," *The Positive Psychlopedia*, May 18, 2016, positivepsychlopedia.com/year-of-happy/benefits-of-flow/.

17. Cal Newport, *Deep Work: Rules for Focused Success in a Distracted World* (New York: GRAND CENTRAL PUB, 2018).

#1 deathbed regret:

"I wish I had the courage to live *a life true to myself,* not the life others expected of me."

soul-satisfying accomplishment. That leads to a range of unhealthy coping behaviors resulting in the rise of chronic disease. The point is that we are designed for and need times of immersive engagement. If you follow your strengths, it will lead you to those sources of deep work, deep love, deep thought, and deep connection.

The connection between the Genius Portrait and the concept of flow should be clear—people experience flow when they are at their best, and their natural qualities and talents, their genius traits, are aligned with the work they are doing and the lives they are living. It's the same experience whether we are talking about our personal lives, our professional roles, or our creative outlets. Clearly, it's tough to imagine Bob or Lilly or Ana experiencing flow and embracing their Genius Spark when their experiences were out of sync with their natural proclivities. That is why it's so important to understand who we are at our best. By writing down a Genius Portrait we have the opportunity to connect our authentic self with the life we are living.

The Power of Mental Rehearsal and Reflection

The term "peak performance" is another concept linked to the idea of flow and the foundation of the Genius Spark. Peak performance science teaches people how to use vivid mental rehearsal to practice and learn. Basically, it focuses on visualization of success in any task. This is a literal practice of the Dale Carnegie quote from earlier in the book: *Whatever the mind can conceive and believe, it can achieve.* When musicians or athletes are asked to think through their routines while in an fMRI machine, they produce the same brain waves as if they were performing the task. Some speakers and coaches misapply this practice only to imagine the end state. The true masters envision the entire process from beginning to end.

Olympic swimmer Michael Phelps provides what I have found to be the most succinct and complete description of the process. In describing his training regimen and recipe for success, Phelps has said, "When I would visualize . . . it would be what you want it to be, what it could be, and what you don't want it to be. You are always ready for whatever comes your way."[18] Basically, Phelps envisions every possible aspect of his challenges and desired outcomes. He sees how success happens, he imagines how things may go wrong and how he would respond, and he visualizes the "best-case" scenario where everything works out optimally.

Great athletes and performers from Michael Jordan to Mikaela Shiffrin are known to practice the art of visualization. In fact, Jordan has written extensively about his mental practice in his book *I Can't Accept Not Trying: Michael Jordan on the Pursuit of Excellence*. In his career, Jordan made the game-winning shot numerous times, and he did so confidently, having first envisioned himself making the shot thousands of times in his mind. That confident approach in which he knows he will succeed applies to not only single shots but his entire career, both on and off the court. "I visualized where I wanted to be, what kind of player I wanted to become. I knew exactly where I wanted to go, and I focused on getting there," says Jordan. [19]

18. Olivier Poirier-Leroy, "How Michael Phelps Used Visualization to Stay Calm Under Pressure," *YourSwimLog.com*, www.yourswimlog.com/michael-phelps-visualization/.

19. Connors, Christopher D. 2018. "The Formula That Leads to Wild Success- Part 1: Michael Jordan." *Medium*, March 26, 2018. https://medium.com/the-mission/the-formula-that-leads-to-wild-success-part-1-michael-jordan-8d3fe552592.

Just like the concept of flow, there is a distinct connection between writing a Genius Portrait and the concepts of visualization and peak performance. The Genius Portrait is a picture of you at your best, a picture you can see every time you read. And that's a practice you should make a daily habit.

Action Step I: Making Your Genius Portrait Visible

Take a tangible step toward embracing your Genius Portrait by making it visible in your daily life. Print it out or write it down and place it where you can easily access it. I have copied mine into the notes app on my phone and read it daily. Whether it's on your bathroom mirror, in your car, or in your wallet, let your portrait serve as a daily reminder of your unique talents and potential. You can even save it digitally and read it aloud directly from your phone or any other device. This personalized affirmation, crafted by you, holds immense power to shape your mindset and actions.

Next, set a reminder on your phone. Seriously, do it right now. Tell your electronic assistant to "remind me every morning at [TIME] to read my Genius Portrait." Because that's what you're going to do: You're going to read your paragraph *out loud* every morning. This is akin to a verbal affirmation or mantra, but unique because you wrote this one yourself. The paragraph isn't some banal platitude. It's not a random inspirational quote that you see on posters in offices and schools. These words are for you, by you.

As you read your own words aloud, I'd encourage you to take a cue from Michael Phelps. You might not be setting world records in the 200m butterfly, but like Phelps, you can use your Genius Portrait to visualize what you want it to be, what you don't want it to be, what it could be. In this case, "it" could be *anything*. "It" might be an upcoming challenging conversation, a crucial meeting, or your overall work day. As you read your paragraph, consider the implications of what you're saying. If those things were true for you today, what would it look, sound, and feel like? This practice may feel unfamiliar at first, but remember that affirming our own excellence is essential before expecting it from others.

Reframing Negative Narratives with Cognitive Behavior Therapy

Dr. Amit Sood addressed a research group I assembled to study the failure of wellness programs to improve health or lower costs. Sood is the Executive Director for the Resilient Option at the Mayo Clinic. Sood's work explains an important insight into understanding how we talk to ourselves—humans are wired to sense danger, and in a modern world, our senses work overtime. In that environment, Sood explained to our group, 80 percent of our undirected thoughts turn negative. We instinctively index toward what is wrong, including how we think of ourselves.

It comes as no surprise, then, that you are probably your harshest critic. When we can't redirect or turn off these thoughts, it can lead to depression and worse. One method the Mayo Clinic uses to change negative thought patterns is Cognitive Behavior Therapy (CBT). Mayo describes the treatment this way: "CBT helps you become aware of inaccurate or negative thinking so you can view challenging situations more clearly and respond to them more effectively."[20] CBT helps to reframe negative narratives and replace them with positive but realistic alternatives.

By implementing a daily practice of reading your Genius Portrait, you can revisit, reinforce, and reflect on your genius traits and, over time, reprogram your thoughts so that your first instincts rely on your talents, and you can begin to value your unique traits. This reframing practice also works in retrospect. We can examine key moments from our past experiences through the new lens of our Genius Portrait.

---

20. "Cognitive Behavioral Therapy," *Mayo Clinic*, March 16, 2019, mayocl.in/44Mt6I8.

Action Step 2: Connecting Past Moments to Your Genius Portrait

Consider a moment from the past week. This could be personal or professional. The best place to start is choosing a time when you felt particularly "on"—firing on all cylinders, effectively. Our goal here is to connect this moment with your Genius Portrait so that we build a new unconscious habit to ascribe these positive moments to something other than serendipity. When we do excellent things, it's because of our inherent excellence. It's not an accident. It's not just good luck. It's the way things are supposed to be when our experience is aligned with our best qualities and traits.

Ask yourself about the *action*, the *origin*, and the *impact* of the moment in question.

Action: What did you *do*, specifically? Use action verbs (kind of like on a resumé). Maybe you *supported* or *guided*, or *designed*.

Origin: What elements of your Genius Portrait came alive at that moment? How did it feel? This can be one of our "aha" moments when we realize that our flow, our success, our optimal performance could be expected because our Genius Portrait frames it that way.

Impact: What was the outcome? For you, for the project, for another person, for a team? It is crucial that we internalize the "so what" of our natural talents and genius traits so we can regularly confirm for ourselves that the outcome, the goal, the success is because of us, not in spite of us.

I would encourage you to use this model regularly to consider moments from your past, both recent and distant. By applying our Genius Portraits in this way, we can continue to expand the depth to which they describes us at our best. This practice will help us develop understanding in the next step of the journey.

Understanding: Until It Really Looks Like You

Jason had been following my instructions diligently. He was reading his Genius Portrait to himself every morning. It had been about six months, and once every couple of weeks or so, I got a text update from him as he had "aha" moments. At one point, Jason was praised for having sat calmly through a contentious meeting and helped both sides of a conflict come to a meaningful solution.

He texted, ". . . and I thought to myself, OF COURSE! MY Genius Portrait says, 'I easily find common ground between opposing viewpoints,' so it makes sense that I was able to do that."

I shared Jason's excitement and recommended he add an addendum to that sentence.

I replied, "I think it might strengthen that sentence if you added, '"I easily find common ground between opposing viewpoints and support people in reaching productive consensus.'"

". . . I can do that?"

YES!

Your Genius Portrait is yours alone. At the time of writing, you likely had a varied understanding of how your core talents show up in your life. After considering it for some time, you will likely have had several experiences confirming or challenging how you've formed your paragraph. This is totally natural and, in fact, is part of the process. By continuing to consider and hone our portrait, we can enhance its descriptive powers and improve how we use it.

Finding FLOW—From Talents to Mastery

Kim naturally turns chaos into order. So, when she showed up to help her daughter organize her apartment, Kim noticed the people standing around with nothing to do. When her daughter asked her to help, she did. "Within ten minutes," Kim told me, "I had everyone putting things in order, and within an hour, we were finished."

I told Kim that story painted a vivid picture of her top trait, Self-Control. She paused, took a breath, and said, "Huh?" Like many leaders, she didn't recognize her strengths. We all send subconscious signals about our genius traits. In my coaching career I've learned to look for enthusiasm, deep listening, high energy, visible frustration, eye rolls, and interruptions. I also learn a lot about individuals by observing their behavior under pressure, moments when they are caught off guard, and backstage behavior, when their audience isn't watching.

After I finished giving Kim a tour through Self-Control, her top trait, I circled back to an off-hand comment she'd made about her trust issues. Trust is a core trait of her second strength, Genuineness. This trait provides a gut-level instinct around trust or distrust.

I said, "You must have a powerful BS meter."

"Absolutely."

"With Self-Control, Genuineness, and Loyalty, I imagine you have a small island of close friends," I suggested.

"It's basically just my husband and me," she explained. "We go to other people's islands."

"So, would I have to take my shoes off when I come into your house?"

"Of course!" I could see she wasn't kidding.

"So, is your closet organized by color and season?"

"I live in Arizona; we basically have one season. But, yes, I have my shirts organized by color."

"And I'm assuming everything has a drawer or place in the pantry where it belongs?"

"We don't have a junk drawer. My slogan is, 'a place for everything and everything in its place.'"

Even though we were talking by Zoom, we found a flow. For an hour, we engaged in conversational jazz, gliding from story to story.

My son Tyler studied jazz, and I played the saxophone years ago. I understand how jazz musicians create what looks like an impromptu performance based on two starting points: the key and a chord progression. An ensemble will first create a musical theme before expanding into creative variations that strike listeners as magical. I also know hours of mastering the fundamentals—scales, arpeggios, chord progressions, transitions, and transpositions—lie behind that deceptively simple opening.

Talents, qualities, and genius traits are like a series of musical notes. The different combinations (arpeggios) and patterns (chord progressions) provide a framework that produces something unique. Just think of the endless variety of songs and compositions built on our eight-note scale. Now imagine working with 20 to 40 notes, the number of talents, that produce a truly unimaginable range of expressions. The better you know and practice your strengths, the easier it is to blend your "style" with others.

Although Kim learned some significant secrets that helped in her career, she seemed more thrilled to see how she and her daughter might flow better together. As a coach, I feel the same way when I see new understanding overflow the banks of the workplace and touch family and community relationships.

If you consider that in one of the well-known psychometric assessments there are 33,600,000 variations of someone's top five talents, you will realize each of us represents a unique melody. And we each carry the ability to create incredible harmony with others. I've also seen intense dissonance when people and conversations fall out of tune. And I've seen people and teams misread a simple tuning problem and turn combative, stuck, and toxic. I've also sometimes seen those same people change, forgive, and become kinder and gentler. I know what it looks like when people learn to appreciate their natural differences and strengths.

Action Step Three: Enhance Your Insights

1. **Celebrate/Acknowledge:** As you reconsider your Genius Portrait, be sure to celebrate and acknowledge the places where it has accurately described you at your best.

2. **Update and Specify:** Like Jason, there will be many opportunities to hone your paragraph to be more specific to your experience. To do that, consider the following questions:

   1. Does my paragraph feel fresh and motivating, or is it starting to feel stale?

   2. If so, is there a second trait or part of one I'd like to add? The Genius Spark app provides eight trait options to choose from for each talent. You can combine two if you feel the combination captures the essence of that talent at its best.

   3. How would I describe a recent peak moment using my talents?

3. **Craft a Counternarrative:** As Sood said, undirected thoughts tend to turn negative. This means that even when we experience positive things, self-doubt can invite us to second-guess ourselves and to create narratives that say our success came from somewhere other than our genius. That's natural. By referring back to our Genius Portrait regularly, we can authentically and honestly redirect our personal storytelling to include ourselves as a factor in our success.

Your Genius Portrait should evolve and change as you build your relationship with it. As your understanding builds, your pattern recognition will improve, and you'll find yourself able to consistently reference your Genius Portrait in healthy and positive ways. Consistent application will enhance your experience.

Action Step Four: Create a Cycle

I have encouraged you to begin a regular practice of considering your Genius Portrait at the start of your day. I believe that will be a rewarding experience. In order to bookend it, I'm now going to suggest a similar practice as a wrap-up to your day or, at the very least, to your week.

At the end of your week, or on an evening that feels like a natural reflection point, take a look at your Genius Portrait. Consider the past several days, and look to connect at least one or two of the sentences from your Genius Portrait to moments from your everyday life. Ideally, jot something down in a journal or ongoing notepad. This might sound something like:

"My genius portrait says I 'lighten the mood when I walk into a room.' I felt this on Tuesday, walking into a meeting everyone knew would be challenging. I know that my presence and effort helped calm people's nerves."

Or:

"I wrote in my Genius Portrait that I 'can pivot quickly when I sense resistance or an obstacle.' This was very apparent on Wednesday when my colleague was concerned about our approach with a specific client. I was able to shift to a new acceptable tactic without much challenge."

Your Genius Spark will always show up because it's just a description of the typical way you approach the world. It's a description of your default behaviors, and it's your job to assess:

1. How did my Genius Portrait line up with my lived experience?
2. Do I categorize my outcomes as positive, negative, or neutral?
3. What alternative or additional outcomes might I hope for next time?
4. What adjustments will I need to make to seek those outcomes?
5. Can I adjust or update my Genius Portrait to be more specific, descriptive, or accurate?

Celebrating and Acknowledging Your Best Self

As we conclude this chapter, we come face-to-face with the profound impact of the Genius Portrait and the initial steps to unleash its power within us. The reactions to discovering our personalized description of our best selves are diverse, ranging from giggles of delight to contemplative silence. We recognize the ownership we have over our paragraphs and the desire to lean into our genius and make it work for us.

The journey toward understanding our Genius Spark leads us to the phase of understanding ourselves. Through anecdotes and stories, we witness individuals like Jason recognizing how their Genius Portraits align with their lived experiences. With time and reflection, our Genius Portraits evolve and change, becoming more descriptive and accurate.

As you reconsider your Genius Portrait, take a moment to celebrate and acknowledge the instances where it accurately describes your best self. It's natural for your paragraph to evolve and potentially feel stale over time. Use this opportunity to update it and add more specific elements that resonate with your experiences. Craft counternarratives to combat negative thoughts and redirect your personal storytelling to include your genius as a driving force behind your success.

As you continue on your journey of self-discovery, unleashing your unique Genius Spark, let your Genius Portrait be a source of inspiration and empowerment. Embrace the endless possibilities of blending your strengths with others, creating harmony and making a positive impact in all aspects of your life. Now, armed with the tools and insights from this chapter, step forward into the next chapter, where we will delve deeper into the transformative power of embracing your unique genius.

Key Lessons from Chapter Five: Visualize, Verbalize, Materialize

1. **Discover your Genius Portrait:** Gain insight into your unique strengths, talents, and traits that describe you at your best.
2. **Embrace your Genius Portrait:** Make it visible in your daily life, reaffirming your strengths and potential.
3. **Practice mental rehearsal and reflection:** Use vivid visualization to mentally rehearse and learn as if you were doing "it," enhancing your performance and mindset.
4. **Craft counternarratives:** Challenge negative thoughts and redirect your personal storytelling to include your genius as a driving force behind your success.
5. **Connect experiences to your Genius Portrait:** Reflect on your everyday experiences and seek connections between your lived experiences and your Genius Portrait, deepening your understanding and making adjustments if needed.
6. **Seek feedback and celebrate your strengths:** Embrace the gift of genuine and specific feedback, acknowledging and celebrating instances where your Genius Portrait accurately describes your best self.
7. **Embrace the transformative power of your unique genius:** Use your Genius Portrait as a compass, guiding you toward self-awareness, growth, and the ability to make a positive impact in all aspects of your life.

Chapter 6

Harnessing the Power of Your Strengths

"To share your weakness is to make yourself vulnerable; to make yourself vulnerable is to show your strength."

—Criss Jami

The Power of Purpose:

Sally, a principal in a 200-person architectural firm,[21] reached out to me through LinkedIn. She leads the corporate interiors practice. Her counterparts lead practices specializing in health care, K12 schools, universities, the federal government, municipalities, commercial developers, and others. The company maintained steady work through the pandemic. However, Sally's practice went into a tailspin because of stay-at-home mandates and the shift to hybrid work. Companies stopped all interior design.

"Rex, I'm burnt out," she told me. "I think I need to do something else. I saw your post on the Genius Spark, and I need some kind of spark to keep going."

---

21. Think of a professional service firm principal as the equivalent of a division president or general manager.

Based on what she described as a typical day, it was no wonder she was running on fumes. Sally had pressure from the firm to maintain billable hours; she dealt with people leaving for more pay or burnout. She told me some of her clients were hiring people out from under her. "A mid-level designer makes $48,000, and my client offered $80,000. How do I compete with that?" Her remaining team was understaffed. Sally spent a lot of time boosting morale or working around individual needs. She worked late at night and got up early. "I have two kids, and I feel so guilty because I'm not showing up as a good mom and wife," she said. "My husband has commented that something has to give."

"You've had your world turned upside down," I told her, "and you're not alone." I then shared my own story of hitting the wall 20 years ago and the promise of a road back. When she finished unloading her burden, I asked two questions.

- What motivates you to get up in the morning?
- Tell me about your sleep. What is your routine?

The answers to these two simple questions have life-changing implications and power. For now, let's focus on the first. I started hearing stories like Sally's as early as May of 2020. Having a clear purpose is one of the disciplines that builds post-traumatic growth. Post-traumatic growth is a set of six traits and practices that allow people to thrive and get stronger when hit with adversity. I begin with purpose because you can't sustain the other disciplines without it.

Post-traumatic growth is the positive psychological changes that can occur following challenging life crises and traumatic events. The concept was pioneered by psychologist Martin Seligman, who found that adversity can lead to a process of building resilience and personal development. People who experience post-traumatic growth emerge with a renewed appreciation for life, a changed sense of priorities, closer relationships, increased personal strength, and deepened spirituality. By applying these principles, we can overcome major setbacks and build the resolve to thrive. Post-traumatic growth provides a framework for harnessing strengths and overcoming weaknesses on the journey to self-actualization.

Our journey began by acknowledging that so many people find themselves all too often in situations where they are being *drained* more than they are being *filled*. They spend more time than they should struggling to apply talents to tasks for which they are not best suited. In the process, they give up more and more of their energy and end up with negative physical and mental health as a result. After that, Sally and I began the process of rediscovering her Genius Spark. We wrote a set of paragraphs to describe ourselves at our best, and stepped into a process and a practice for moving from the drain zone to the flow zone. In the flow zone we are effectively and appropriately leveraging our talents to great effect. But there is one more zone that we must be aware of: our kryptonite zone.

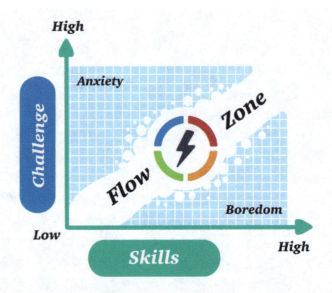

Kryptonite and the Anti-Flow: When Our Traits Go South

Each of our natural talents and genius traits has a "shadow side," our kryptonite, which can lead to unintended, and potentially negative, consequences. It's important to reiterate here: Your traits and talents are your defaults. They represent the strongest neurological pathways in your brain. Whether appropriate for the situation or not, they are likely to be the talents you lean on to approach most situations in your life. Your brain is so accustomed to leaning into these talents that when you apply them, it will release dopamine, signaling that, "You're doing great; you're doing a thing that you're good at, so keep doing that thing!"

Your brain can sometimes continue to feed you this message even as you move further and further from your goal. The potential dangers from kryptonite align with how we often experience the shadow side of our talents. The path toward understanding these dangers and responding effectively to their potential impacts is the next one that we will travel together.

First, we must be just as aware of what our kryptonite looks like as our genius traits and under what circumstances those shadow traits typically surface. Next, we have to understand the varying degrees of kryptonite we typically experience, or perhaps cause those around us to experience. Finally, we must guard against the potential impacts of our own individual kryptonite zone.

Navigating the Zones: From Drain to Flow to Kryptonite

The neurological waterways that represent our natural talents and genius traits are the widest, deepest, and fastest flowing pathways in our brain. They are the paths we most often navigate toward a desired outcome, but they also present the most likely place where we will get in our own way. Under pressure we can push out talents beyond their sweet spot. We can get caught up in our talents and lose touch with how we come across to others. Finally, we can consciously or unconsciously shut down one or more talents because of negative experiences in the past.

I've noticed this pattern in myself. When conducting a workshop, part of my magic is creating a one-off experience. I start with a loose agenda and framework and rely on my experience to adapt to the audience's interest and energy. I see patterns at a high level and enjoy balancing creating individual aha moments, staying close to the schedule and finishing with a climactic call to action. I can get so wrapped up in this process that I skip details important to others or change directions without explaining why. One of my kryptonite traits is that I assume what is clear to me is clear to you. At the beginning of a workshop, I share what I hope to accomplish through my genius traits but where I might need help if my kryptonite shows up.

My son coined a phrase to describe when this happens: "Dad, you dusted me." He came up with this after a workshop when he shared that sometimes I leave people in the dust, including himself. That's when I need help, and a simple phrase like, "Rex, you dusted me," breaks me from my dopamine trance, inserts humor, and allows me to reset. When I do this, it also models how to acknowledge and learn from my kryptonite to be an effective leader, team member, or family member.

Understanding How Our Traits Can Work Against Us

The principle behind a kryptonite trait begins by pushing a genius trait to an extreme, losing awareness of how others are experiencing us or when a trait deactivates or shuts down. Over time you'll see patterns, situations, or people that trigger these responses. It's almost as if each sentence in our Genius Portrait had a big "but" added to the end.

Consider this sentence from Ana's Genius Portrait in Chapter 4:

"I like to start with the end in mind and work my way backward."

This is Ana's first sentence in her portrait. It's likely her go-to talent when approaching anything. Professionally, Ana's desk is full of timelines and project plans. Ana can create a checklist from beginning to end. When creating her Kryptonite Portrait, her job is to consider the following:

By insisting on starting with the end and working my way backward, what might I miss, misinterpret, or mistake?

To start answering this question, add a "but":

"I like to start with the end in mind and work my way backward BUT . . ."

- I sometimes get caught up in planning and need to pay more attention to immediate execution.

or

- I can get impatient when I'm ready to move on, and others get further into the weeds.

or

- I can be narrow-minded about potentially good ideas that don't fit directly into the end that I have in mind.

Ana's strategic mind can be a great asset *or* a cause of the challenge, and this reframing of her Genius Portrait gives her a chance to catalog that and put it on paper.

Here is Ana's entire Kryptonite Portrait:

"I can get impatient when I'm ready to move on, and others get further into the weeds. Not everyone appreciates my attempts to coach or develop them. In my eagerness to 'get something started,' I can ignore the feelings and anxieties of others. In my haste to distill and synthesize information, I can leave out important details that seem inconsequential. I have to schedule downtime to avoid burnout."

Much like the genius side of our Genius Portrait, our priorities for our Kryptonite Portrait are, in order, Language, Insights, and Energy. We must be able to describe the shadow sides of our talents so that we can be aware of them. Superman cannot rid the world of all kryptonite any more than we can stop ourselves from leaning too far into our core talents. It's going to happen; our goal is to understand when it's most likely to happen and the impact it's likely to have.

You'll notice that this paragraph reads less like an indictment than a precautionary statement. Almost as if to say, "if I'm *not* aware of these tendencies, this can happen as a result." This declaration is crucial because it signals that we need not feel shame around the impact of our kryptonite, and our magic only grows along with our understanding of it.

Noticing Differences: Recognizing Complementary Styles and Potential Frictions

If you see two ring patterns that are distinctly different it's a clue of how the styles complement one another. It is also a clue of where they can run into friction. Most conflict situations I'm brought into end up being two people with differing dominant zones. It is as if they speak different languages. They see the same situation and draw different conclusions. On more than one occasion I've been able to identify the root issue between two people within the first five minutes by looking at their different ring patterns.

In one case a project manager was convinced his general superintendent was insubordinate and attempted to sabotage the $350 million dollar project. On the surface that seems implausible. The general superintendent has far more to lose than gain by undermining the project, unless the animosity was so high that he was simply out for revenge. There were no signs that was the case.

The project manager could not see the situation any other way until I compared their rings and held my ground that there was an alternative explanation. After about 45 minutes of venting he relented and I shared the following.

"Mike, you are all action and have no core Thinking traits. When you're under stress you go from action to reaction. Jason, on the other hand, has no Acting traits, but his Thinking zone is incredible. He doesn't react and certainly does not feel compelled to do something just because you're angry or demanding. He analyzes, considers the implications, and looks for the most efficient solution. The two of you couldn't be more different and if you can work out your differences, you're a perfect team."

Mike dropped his head and repeated, "I've effed up" over and

"The creative adult is the child who survived."

- Ursula K. LeGuin

over. We called Jason into the conference room and Mike gave a heartfelt apology that turned emotional for all of us. The two of them spent some time together to restore their trust and explore how they could work as a team.

In the evening the leadership for the project met for submarine sandwiches, chips and sodas. The general mood was unengaged and awkward chitchat. The team had been split in half siding with either Mike or Jason. The construction trailer had become a warzone cordoned off depending on whose side you were on.

Mike and Jason asked for a moment to speak together. They shared how the pressures of the project and their blind spots created misunderstanding and animosity, leading to them becoming adversaries. This tension had been going on for almost a year.

The team was caught off guard by the sudden positive change between the two. I was able to project Mike and Jason's ring patterns on the wall and explain how they spoke different languages, saw things differently, and how their talents turned to blind spots and weaknesses under pressure. Their willingness to not insist on being right but rather how to be effectively shifted was a turning point for the project.

When I go into conflict situations like this I only know what I am told about the problem. I am never sure what to expect or how people will react. When I first started in this work, I dreaded these encounters. I still feel anxious, but after working through hundreds of conflicts there are recurring themes, skills to de-escalate, and strategies to improve the odds of resolution.

Kryptonite and Conflict: Lessons for Conflict Resolution

In addition to using ring patterns and walking through the Genius Spark system, here are some lessons I'd like to pass along.

- In most cases those in conflict want the same thing: a successful project or relationship. I often have to ask the parties involved, "Do you want to be right or effective?"
- Each party assumes what is clear to them is clear to the other.
- When there is miscommunication or misalignment, it is common to have different dominant zones, speaking different languages.
- Traits can also collide, either directly or because they fall on another end of the spectrum.
- If there is one common thread, people in conflict create a story about the other person without verifying their assumptions. I use the acronym NIMSU to describe this: No Information, Make Stuff Up.

Vulnerability and Connection: Sharing Strengths and Kryptonite

So far, we've only discussed how you might, on an individual basis, find utility in the analysis and awareness of your genius. Leveraging the Genius Sparks of multiple people on a team or at an organization is something I'll cover in greater depth in another text. However, once you've composed *both* your Genius Portrait and your Kryptonite Portrait, it can be incredibly beneficial to share them with others. Just as clear language can help us notice our tendencies, so can it help assist others. This practice can strengthen our relationships, deepen our dialogues, and create connections in unexpected places.

I worked with a manager named Jared who struggled to sort out why his direct reports seemed to avoid coming to him with new ideas. I counseled him to set up an open conversation with one of his staff about his Genius Portrait, specifically the kryptonite side.

Jared was nervous. This conversation felt like a vulnerable activity, and he was worried about this degree of openness with his staff. I asked him, "Is there anything you've written in your kryptonite paragraph that isn't true?"

"No," he acknowledged with a sheepish sort of smile.

"Alright then, here's how you set it up. Tell your staff member that you're looking for feedback, that you'd like to read them a paragraph, and ask them to think of times when they've seen these types of tendencies in you as a leader and colleague. Your job isn't to respond; just listen for right now."

Jared was nervous but agreed. About a week later, I received an excited phone call. Jared had shared his kryptonite paragraph with a colleague, and they immediately picked up on the second sentence:

- "My questioning and skepticism can make conversations about new ideas difficult."

Jared said he didn't even have to ask a prompting question. When he read that sentence out loud, his staff member chuckled, seeing it immediately as reflective of their experience with Jared. It turns out that Jared's analytical mind, which was constantly assessing costs, benefits, risks, and rewards, was being experienced by his staff as quickly rejecting their ideas. Jared told me that since that conversation, he has taken more time in meetings to listen rather than evaluate. New ideas had a place at the table, and tension on his team had dissipated.

Jared didn't stop using his natural talents and traits. He's still evaluating new ideas analytically. It's just that now he's added some awareness of how that talent might impact the people around him and is more conscious of its application. The power of our paragraphs, both of them, is that *we* wrote them. They can't exist unless we agree that they are accurate. If they don't feel authentic, we have more work to do; see Chapter 4 again.

I recommend sharing your paragraphs—both of them—with people you know well—co-workers, colleagues, family, and friends. Ask people these questions.

1. Which of these sentences and descriptors ring most true when you think about me?
2. When do you see them the most?
3. When these qualities or traits show up, what are some common outcomes?

Your role is listening and asking people to expand on their comments. The conversations should feel a little one-sided. Look for 'aha' moments and confirmation and clarification for how you've described yourself.

Reflecting for Growth: Harnessing Insights from Kryptonite

I told you to print your Genius Portrait, reflect on it daily, and read it aloud to yourself regularly. Our Kryptonite Portrait is different. Rather than ruminate on how our talents can sabotage us, I recommend a monthly check-in with your kryptonite in which you ask yourself these three questions.

1. Where in the last month has my kryptonite shown up? This could be personally or professionally.
2. How aware was I when it was happening? Did I notice this at the time, or only now, upon reflection?

3. What impact did it have on the space or people around me? This impact may not be massive or even particularly damaging. It's just important to acknowledge the way that our tendencies affect the things around us.

This regular reflection allows you to revise and revitalize your kryptonite paragraphs. Just like your Genius Portrait, the goal is that this description is as true as it can be for you.

Embracing Heroic Alter Egos: Tapping into Inspirational Avatars

William James, the father of modern psychology, said, "If you want a quality, act as if you already have it." Bill Wilson, the Alcoholics Anonymous founder, agreed. He said, "It's easier to act your way into a new way of thinking than to think your way into a new way of acting." In his book, *The As If Principle* (Simon & Schuster, 2014), Richard Wiseman presented research about the power of body language and physical actions, confirming that if people smile and cross their arms, it doubles the time they can persevere at a given task. Other research validated that making a fist gives you 40 percent more willpower.

Similarly, in Amy Cuddy's book, *Presence* (Little, Brown Spark, 2015), she unpacks the chemical boost you get by just taking a power pose, the Wonder Woman stance. When Harvard psychology professor Ellen Langer brought people in their 70s and 80s into a room with décor and music from an earlier era, they stood straighter, displayed improved memories, developed stronger muscle tone, and behaved as if they were 10 years younger.[22] Langer conducted another experiment that showed a marked im-

22. Bruce Grierson, "What If Age Is Nothing but a Mind-Set?" *The New York Times*, October 22, 2014, www.nytimes.com/2014/10/26/magazine/what-if-age-is-nothing-bu t-a-mind-set.html.

Visualize Your Genius Portrait

provement in vision in a group of ROTC candidates who wanted to become pilots.[23] When the candidates were divided into two groups, one group was told nothing, and the other group was asked to imagine they were already Air Force pilots. After a series of tests, 40 percent of the second group showed improved vision.

One helpful technique for keeping our Genius Portrait present in our minds and in our lives is to choose a heroic alter ego character as an avatar. Consider these examples:

One manager with a Servant Leader ring has traits like Genuineness, Drive, Loyalty, Curiosity and a sense of Purpose. He chose Captain Miller from the movie *Saving Private Ryan* as his alter ego. He told our team, "Miller was just a high school English teacher there to do a job and keep his platoon safe."

An executive assistant with an Energizer ring—her traits are

23. "Do You Really Need Those Eyeglasses?" *Association for Psychological Science - APS*, April 2, 2010, www.psychologicalscience.org/news/were-only-human/do-you-really-need-those-eyeglasses.html.

Persuasion, Optimism, Visionary, sense of Purpose, and Genuineness—chose Mary Poppins. She loves the character because of her poise under pressure and her wit.

I recently met with an executive with a Sage ring who dialed in on one strength, Genuineness. He selected Jack Byrnes (Robert De Niro) from the movie *Meet the Fockers.* He just said, "Circle of trust!" while mimicking De Niro's gesture of taking two fingers to his eyes and then turning them toward me.

These steps build knowledge and a deeper understanding of what we look like at our best. The next step is to create awareness of how our strengths look and feel in real-time.

The On and Off Switch:
Leveraging Strengths and Recognizing Limits

Virginia—a single mom, ex-soldier, and part of a toxic team of engineers—worked hard to turn off her empathetic radar and amp up some of her other strengths for combat mode.

When she first read the descriptions of her top five strengths, she said, "There's no way I have Emotional Awareness. I don't do Emotional Tune-ins." When I first met Virginia the morning of the workshop, I also had my doubts. She lived up to the descriptions I had heard. But the dilemma activated my curiosity, and I led with that hat. I hit everyone with Vigilance first, which was the most common strength on the team. Those with Vigilance were the most skeptical, so I asked the team to share stories of a time when their Vigilance saved the day.

I went down the list of strengths from the most common to the least. Then I hit Emotional Awareness. Three people had the trait, and all went well until I came to Virginia. She wore a tight-lipped scowl and called me out.

"This is garbage, 'Emotional Awareness'?! Ha! That is definitely NOT on the top of my list"

"Okay, Virginia, maybe the assessment got it wrong, but let me ask a question. Do you have any kids?"

"Yes, my daughter who goes to Tulane. She's home on break."

"Nice, and what is your relationship like?"

"We're tight!"

"How tight?"

"I know exactly what is going on inside her before she steps into my kitchen."

"Wow, how do you know?"

"I just do; I always have."

"So, Virginia, Emotional Awareness allows you to sense your daughter's feelings, to put yourself in her shoes. It's not about being soft or emotional. Does that make sense?"

Virginia leaned back, arms folded, and nodded. She didn't say anything, but something big was clearly happening.

Virginia went back to read more about the Emotional Awareness trait with a new open mind. She understood it, embraced it, and owned it. She asked her executive officer if she could be the team's champion for strengths. Virginia helped the team turn around and go from toxic to inspired to learn more about their strengths and colleagues.

Think about some activities you enjoy most and those you try to avoid. Compare them to your strengths. Consider what turns them on and off. Like Virginia, you might have turned off one or more of your strengths and perhaps are overcompensating with other strengths.

If you feel engaged and happy in an activity, it's a good sign you are playing to some of your strengths. If you feel uninterested or stressed, that may show you've turned off your top strengths.

The Genius Spark helps connect physical and emotional energy to your traits. It can help you understand why you feel engaged in some situations and uninterested or stressed in others and how to shift that energy.

Key Lessons from Chapter Six:
Harnessing the Power of your Strengths

1. **The Importance of Purpose:** Having a clear sense of purpose is crucial for sustaining personal growth and overcoming challenges.

2. **Understanding the Drain, Flow, and Kryptonite Zones:** People can find themselves in the "drain zone" when tasks are mismatched with their strengths, while the "flow zone" arises when core talents are effectively utilized for success, and the "kryptonite zone" signifies the adverse outcomes of either excessive or misguided application of strengths.

3. **Building a Kryptonite Portrait:** By identifying and understanding our kryptonite traits, we can mitigate their negative impacts and foster personal growth.

4. **The Power of Sharing Strengths and Shadows:** Sharing our Genius and Kryptonite Portraits with others can strengthen relationships, deepen dialogue, and create unexpected connections.

5. **Reflecting on Kryptonite for Growth:** This reflection process increases self-awareness and enables us to address weaknesses and mitigate their negative effects.

6. **Embracing Heroic Alter Egos:** Adopting heroic alter egos as avatars can provide inspiration and motivation to unleash our full potential.

7. **Leveraging Strengths and Recognizing Limits:** Understanding when to utilize our strengths and acknowledging their limitations is crucial for personal and professional growth.

Chapter 7

Igniting Potential with the Genius Spark

"Your potential is the thing you haven't done yet."

—Unknown

Jim was a construction project manager with over 20 years of experience. He had a reputation for delivering successful projects, but lately felt overwhelmed and exhausted. No matter how hard he worked, it never seemed to be enough. His team depended on him to resolve conflicts, motivate everyone, and drive performance.

The constant firefighting left little time for Jim to focus on strategic priorities or his own development. He desperately needed more balance and support. There had to be a better way than shouldering so much responsibility alone.

Under the stress of falling behind, Jim's strong trait of Reliability took the lead, and he took on more responsibility. His over-performance took the pressure off the team, and they were happy to let Jim own the success or failure of the project. However, it was crucial for him to realign ownership with the entire team, rebuild the trust that had eroded due to project delays, and establish a new understanding regarding each member's contribution to the team's triumph. This entailed shifting the focus from individual roles and emphasizing collective success.

That's when Jim stumbled upon the Genius Spark—a game-changer. Rather than a generalized analysis, the Genius Spark software provided customized insights into each team member's unique strengths and potential blind spots. The process illuminated how different personalities and reactions contributed to escalating team conflicts. But the true power was in the next step. The Genius Spark walked each person through crafting a personalized paragraph describing themselves at their best. Sharing these Genius Portraits shifted the team's focus away from flaws and toward harnessing everyone's individual talents and passions. Where there had been dysfunction, now there was possibility. By revealing each member's inner genius, the tool helped transform both team dynamics and results.

Moreover, the exercise of sharing each person's kryptonite paragraph worked wonders in smoothing the naturally occurring friction among diverse personalities. It created a safe space for constructive feedback, fueling better dialogue and more productive debates during construction issue meetings.

Considering the project was already under strict cost scrutiny, the cost of the Genius Spark and the fact that Jim could lead the conversation within a few hours, instead of needing to hire an expensive consultant for a full-day workshop, made it an affordable and efficient solution. The investment in both the system and the saved time proved invaluable in getting the team back on track.

Like Jim, managers everywhere struggle with a lack of ownership, continuous conflict, and burnout. The Genius Spark offers a proven solution focusing on individual strengths and sustainable growth. Let's explore the unique features and benefits that set this system apart.

What Every Organization Wants

As a consultant, I've covered the vast landscape of American business, industry, education, architecture, commercial construction, health care, and other disciplines for over a quarter-century. Each organization I've worked with is searching for the following.

1. A common language to work better together and enhance their culture
2. A simple and reliable process to release and optimize each person's magic
3. Insight to improve how people perform under pressure and with others
4. Understanding how to motivate individuals and teams toward fuller engagement
5. Developing a process to scale these skills through the organization and culture

What Stands In the Way?

Every assessment offers a common language for users to understand themselves and their co-workers, but only if a company uses one system. Several large organizations I work with may use DISC in some field offices, Myers Briggs at the corporate level, and StrengthsFinder for projects and teams. Recently, Enneagram has become popular as well.

Most assessments reveal unique insights about one's personality or talents. The Genius Spark starts with those results and insights to guide people and teams in creating a short, simple portrait of their true potential. The Genius Spark online training and tools build on this unique portrait to guide individuals and teams toward mastery and provide managers with a process to develop their teams into high performers.

The insights these assessments offer require expensive licensing fees and consultant engagements, limiting access. As a result, only select groups in an organization typically participate. The Genius Spark removes these barriers through a simplified strengths discovery process and an affordable subscription model. This allows individuals at *all* levels to benefit from strengths development, not just executives.

Democratizing Development

I have worked with the leadership team of a large distribution company for several years, using a variety of assessment tools. They appreciate and are impressed with my ability to help their leaders work better together. When I unpack individual and team profiles, they describe the way I can describe someone so accurately without knowing them as feeling like a magic trick.

In the hands of a skilled consultant, that is exactly how it looks and feels, but it shouldn't be that way. The company has struggled to create a common language and help people perform at their best for all the reasons I outlined above until now. The first Genius Spark workshop I provided to the leadership team created some of the most engaging, heartfelt, and vulnerable conversations they had experienced.

We created their portraits together in the conference room and read them aloud. Instead of feeling analyzed, they felt humanized and proud of the description they wrote of their unique contributions to the team and company. These senior leaders said the Genius Spark provided a powerful experience, gave insight into people's magic, and was easy enough for any manager in their organization to use.

Using the Genius Spark to cascade training to their warehouse workers and delivery drivers created a culture of equity and empowerment across the company, not just for a privileged few. Unlocking potential at every level creates a multiplier effect because every employee is aware of their strengths and potential, not just management. This development was a game changer in their professional development and workplace culture

Like most companies, their approach to talent development had involved complex assessments, generic training, and little follow-through. Employees came out of occasional workshops motivated but quickly reverted to old habits. That changed when the company adopted the Genius Spark. The simplified process, ongoing reinforcement, and inclusive accessibility ignited their workforce in new ways—from the warehouse floor to the executive suites.

Here are a few sparks that catalyzed their success:

- Common Language: Genius Portraits gave everyone a shared vocabulary to appreciate each other's strengths. This built connection and teamwork.
- Daily Exercises: Short Genius Spark warm-ups at the start of meetings, rather than a twice-a-year workshop, kept development top of mind.
- Internal Certification: With affordable in-house Genius Spark guides, they could customize training and meet growing demand.
- Constructive Feedback: Employees proactively resolve conflicts using techniques to frame issues through a strengths lens.
- Role Tailoring: Managers optimized talent by reviewing team data and aligning assignments to maximize strengths fit.
- Accessibility: Ongoing reinforcement became seamless with the Genius Spark web app's bite-sized training and reflection prompts.

Outdated training models will not develop the workforce needed to thrive amid industry disruption. When they tapped into their unlimited human potential by embracing the Genius

Spark's reimagined approach, employees gained a stronger sense of purpose and became partners in the company's success.

Transferring Ownership and Reducing Drama

Ongoing reinforcement is where the magic happens with strengths development. But traditional programs lack tools and support for sustainability. The initial workshop ends, and months later, nothing has fundamentally changed.

The Genius Spark equips managers to take ownership by embedding growth into regular routines with an intuitive and accessible web platform, bite-sized training, reflection exercises, and team meeting catalysts. Instead of isolated events, development integrates seamlessly into each week. For instance, weekly Genius Spark exercises helped construction teams start meetings with a quick warm-up focused on strengths. This small habit kept their Genius Portraits top of mind and improved communication.

Unresolved conflicts place heavy demands on managers' time and energy. Constant mediation leaves little room for strategic leadership. The Genius Spark contains powerful features to defuse drama and promote healthy resolution. The Bridging Differences tool guides employees to address issues directly by highlighting strengths. Peer-to-peer recognition helps positive behaviors overshadow negative ones.

A hospital system reported that nurses used the Genius Spark techniques to reduce tension and solve interpersonal problems themselves instead of escalating them. This freed up managers to coach and develop employees, rather than referee conflicts.

More for Less

A client called and asked me to deliver a partnering workshop for 106 people on a large construction project. They showed interest in the Genius Spark but were already using another system. My quote to lead the workshop using the Genius Spark appealed to them. Still, managers expressed concern about introducing a new approach to a team that had already received training in the other system. I understood.

Over the years, I have run into that same objection, demonstrating this other system to new prospects. Generally, their hesitance around change sounds like this: "We love the insights you've provided, but we're standardized on another system, and we don't want to confuse people". I designed the Genius Spark to unify the collage of assessments and democratize access with a low-cost bridge between them.

They wanted to know how to keep 106 people engaged for a day and not create confusion with a new system. The incentive to save money on the Genius Spark was enticing enough to conduct a virtual test workshop with team members. Here is what we learned through that experience:

1. The Genius Spark built on the work the team had previously done. It did not feel like a new system.
2. We opened with a recap of what they had learned in the first workshop. After six months with no interim training or coaching, the participants had vague recollections of the training and were not putting it to work.
3. The process of creating and sharing their paragraphs generated more energy and engagement with one another than in the previous training.
4. The participants deeply appreciated each person's "magic." Instead of hearing someone say, "I'm a high D with a secondary S," or "I have Discipline® and Adaptability®," people shared a unique and personal paragraph about what they look like at their best that was easy to relate to. Translating abstract traits into short Genius Portraits humanized the results and made them memorable.

The same level of engagement happened during the partnering workshop. People felt the process was intuitive, and their portraits reflected their best traits. It was easier to see what was behind each colleague's "magic," and easy to share and use each person's portrait to improve communication.

Because of the workshop's success, several participants asked how they could introduce the Genius Spark to their companies. The construction firm that organized the workshop asked for a price comparison of what they had spent over the last two years using the other system, and it totaled $120,000 before the coaching and consulting. The Genius Spark would have been under $20,000, including online training and the weekly forums.

I traveled back two months later to expand the work for that project and introduce it to another construction project team that had heard about the experience.

Matching Talent to Roles

Managers often struggle to properly assess talent and identify the best roles for a given individual. The Genius Spark's integrated feedback and planning tools close this gap.

Managers can review individual and team data to make informed decisions about development areas, work style compatibility, and high-potential candidates for new initiatives. Placing people where they can thrive unlocks discretionary effort and excellence.

For example, a sales VP used her team's Genius Portraits to tailor coaching and to help each salesperson better understand their unique approach to success. While one salesperson learned why they were a natural networker, another, equally successful, had an uncanny knack for coming up with novel solutions to client problems. This targeted development helped the company exceed its revenue goals.

Leadership Development

Only 18 percent of managers have a natural strength for developing others. Most focus on tasks over team empowerment, contributing to disengagement.[24] The Genius Spark builds critical coaching and mentoring skills through modeling, practice, and reinforcement. The training pathways guide managers from self-awareness to understanding others to foster group success.

The CEO of a prominent global construction firm took a bold step by leading a Genius Spark exercise during an offsite leadership retreat. Initially, he had requested a consultant's presence for facilitation. However, witnessing the consultant effortlessly demonstrate the ease of using and developing teams with the Genius Spark, the CEO expressed his interest in giving it a try himself. The exercise proved to be highly successful, with the added benefit of saving the company $8,000 that would have otherwise been spent on an external consultant.

Strengths-Based Culture

Workplace trends like remote work, job-switching, and automation require organizations to better engage employees as individuals. But building connections and shared culture with dispersed teams is extremely hard.

The Genius Spark develops a cohesive culture by revealing the humanity and potential in every employee. Seeing colleagues through a strengths lens fosters trust, appreciation, and unity. The result is that people give their best effort because they feel valued for who they are.

Companies using the Genius Spark report that team members know each other on a much deeper level and recognize their coworkers' genius. This strengthens camaraderie, empathy, and retention.

24. Randall Beck and Jim Harter, "Why Great Managers Are so Rare," April 19, 2023, www.gallup.com/workplace/231593/why-great-managers-rare.aspx.

Continuous Evolution

While foundational strengths remain steady, how we apply them must evolve with personal growth and changing environments. The Genius Spark is designed for flexibility. Individuals can continue to clarify and expand their Genius Portrait. The system also adds new training modules and features regularly based on the latest research. Ongoing enhancement keeps development fresh and relevant.

For example, recent Genius Spark additions like the peer recognition tool, virtual workshop capabilities, and team conflict resolution templates keep participants engaged over the long haul. The Genius Spark delivers several unique benefits:

- *Accessible, affordable development for all employees*
- *Tools and reinforcement for sustainable change*
- *Constructive ways to minimize team conflict*
- *Matching talent to roles for optimal performance*
- *Building coaching and mentoring skills in managers*
- *A strengths-based culture that engages employees*
- *Flexibility and continuous evolution of the system*

While problems persist and new challenges keep emerging, your team's potential remains constant. The Genius Spark is the catalyst to ignite that potential and channel it toward excellence. Let the sparks fly!

Your organization likely faces challenges reaching, engaging, and advancing employees at scale. The Genius Spark can become your spark. Let it ignite a culture that unlocks the talent, passion, and creativity already present on your teams. The only limits are the ones we impose on ourselves.

Jim's Journey with the Genius Spark

Jim, the burnt-out construction project manager from the opening of this chapter, carried the weight of his team's performance alone. Exhausted and overwhelmed, he saw no way out. But discovering the Genius Spark gave Jim hope for transforming his situation and leadership abilities. He knew it could guide his team members to unlock their potential and reduce his burden. Here is what Jim's journey looked like over the next 12 months:

Month 1—Jim completes his individual Genius Spark assessment and builds his personal Portrait. The process gives him clarity on his natural talents and growth opportunities.

Month 2—Jim learns how to facilitate his team through the Genius Spark Discovery Session. They gain insights about themselves and each other by creating Portraits.

Month 3—Regular Genius Spark exercises help the team apply their strengths in daily interactions and tasks. Jim also uses insights to tailor his coaching approach to individuals.

Month 6—With the techniques learned through the Genius Spark, his team proactively resolves conflicts. Jim spends less time meditating and puts more focus on mentoring high-potential employees.

Month 9—Jim completes the Genius Spark Leadership Mastery program. He can now foster an autonomous yet collaborative team culture.

Month 12—Jim's team has become self-motivated and handles almost all conflicts independently. He devotes time to strategic priorities instead of constant firefighting.

With the Genius Spark's guidance, Jim transformed into the leader he always wanted to be. He developed new abilities to empower his team and realized his full potential along the way. The results speak for themselves—happier, healthier, and more successful teams.

Your organization may be facing challenges similar to Jim's. But take that first step, and the Genius Spark can help write your success story too. The journey begins from within.

"*Every child is born blessed with a vivid imagination. But just as a muscle grows flabby with disuse, so the bright imagination of a child pales in later years if he ceases to exercise it.*"

- Walt Disney

Key Lessons for Chapter Seven: Igniting Potential with the Genius Spark

1. **Equity and Inclusion through Affordable Access:** Genius Spark democratizes development through affordable access for all employees. This promotes equity and inclusion.
2. **Transfer of Ownership and Ongoing Engagement:** The web app platform and bite-sized exercises transfer ownership from consultants to internal leaders and managers. There is ongoing engagement and reinforcement beyond one-time workshops.
3. **Reducing Conflict Through Feedback:** Constructive feedback techniques reduce team conflict by framing issues through a strengths lens. This minimizes drama that managers must mediate.
4. **Optimizing Talent Allocation:** Managers can optimize talent allocation through insights on individual and team abilities from Genius Spark data. People are matched to the right roles.
5. **Developing Managerial Skills:** Leadership training pathways develop coaching, mentoring, and team empowerment skills in managers. Few managers naturally excel at developing others without this guidance.
6. **Fostering Trust and Empathy:** A strengths-based work culture fosters deeper understanding between colleagues. This leads to greater trust, empathy, and retention.
7. **Continuous Evolution for Relevance:** Continuous evolution of Genius Spark features and resources keeps the development journey fresh and relevant over time. The system adapts to changing needs.

Mastery Starts with Your Genius Portrait

"The only journey is the one within."

—Rainer Maria Rilke

Crafting our Genius Portrait is the first step to recapturing the traits we lost and left behind that make us unique and happy. It is the first step to understanding what we look like at our best and realizing our full potential. But we can't end the story here.

During the COVID-19 pandemic I coached more than 100 leaders. Many struggled at different times. When someone hit a low point I asked, "What gets you up in the morning?" Or, "What's your purpose?" Not one of those 100+ people was able to share their purpose with me. Not one person had a clear answer. Their happiness depended on external conditions outside their control. Their happiness depended on arriving someplace in life: a promotion, a fulfilling project, retirement, a successful company, seeing colleagues daily, travel, or any number of external rewards or achievements.

These coaching sessions fueled me to complete my work on the Genius Spark and help people answers questions like:

- *What's my purpose?*
- *How do I fulfill it?*
- *How can I get closer each day toward fulfilling my purpose?*

Your Universal Purpose—A Vision of Your Best Self

Abraham Maslow, the great-granddad of positive psychology, said, "What a man can be, he must be."[25] You and I have a common need: the quest to become our best selves. That journey is vital to finding happiness.

Psychologist Carl Rogers emphasizes that the secret is in how you approach the journey. "The good life is a process, not a state of being." [26]The level of our engagement is what determines happiness, not the end state. When we lack clarity about our purpose, we don't learn the small daily lessons we encounter when on the

Don't Start Here

WHY

Start Here

WHO
you really are

WHERE
you belong

WHAT
you contribute

path to becoming our best selves. One mentor told me, "It's not about keeping your eye on the prize; it's about keeping your eye on the path."

A results mindset has been my lifelong Achilles heel. From the time I was a child, I've been the person always asking, "Are we there yet?" Many of the people I coach can relate. Our fixation on immediate results sends us on a circular journey that leaves us learning lessons over and over again, the hard way. It's taken me a long time to incorporate consistent mindfulness practices and work on remaining present when everything in me wants just to get there. I use a simple metaphor from

---

25. Maslow, Abraham H. 1993. *The Farther Reaches of Human Nature.* Penguin Books.

26. Rogers, C. R. (1961). On becoming a person. Boston, MA: Houghton Mifflin.

teacher Tal Ben-Shahar that has given me a valuable weapon to defeat this foe: Consider the vision of your best self to become a guiding star, not a distant shore.

From Extrinsic to Intrinsic Motivation

Ancient wisdom and positive psychology agree that flourishing comes from within. It is intrinsic. Dr. Martin Seligman, an early leader in the world of positive psychology, led a diverse research team to identify character traits valued by all cultures and that individuals across cultures found to be self-motivating. The team compared these to the virtues outlined in eight major wisdom traditions, producing a detailed taxonomy of character strengths, as well as a free assessment like the ones I've mentioned throughout this book.

Virtues are the core characteristics valued by moral philosophers and religious thinkers: wisdom, courage, humanity, justice, temperance, and transcendence. These six broad categories of virtue emerge consistently from historical surveys. "We argue that these are universal, perhaps grounded in biology through an evolutionary process that selected for the aspects of excellence as a means of solving the important tasks necessary for survival of the species."[27]

The psychometric assessments identify your talent potential. Seligman's Virtue in Action assessment identifies your top character strengths. Mastery and virtue are two sides to the same coin, with mastery being the 'superior development and application of your talents' and virtue being 'the application of your talents, such as they are, to the pursuit of superior ends (for yourself or for others). You can arrive at the same place building from either direction, but using both adds clarity and a deeper understanding of the best version of yourself. And, the stronger your understanding of your strengths, the more powerfully you can apply those strengths in the pursuit of virtuous ends. I will

---

27. Christopher Peterson, *Character Strengths and Virtues* (Oxford: Oxford University Press, 2004).

share an example of moving from strengths to virtues in a story about Dave.

Distilling Your Go-To Strength

In one workshop, I led a team in developing their Genius Portraits. Then we read the paragraphs aloud and allowed others to comment and share stories of seeing one another at their best. That portion of the workshop was very helpful, even emotionally stirring for some.

Dave, the "backbone" of the team with a Servant Leader ring, was reserved. He sat deep in a wicker chair on the back deck of one of our training facilities as he read his portrait. He laid his portrait on his lap when finished, ready for the next person to share. But not so fast. I asked the team if they had a story that reflected what Dave had just read.

Every person on the team had a behind-the-scenes heroic story about Dave. After about 10 minutes of stories and commentaries, the buzz subsided, and Dave was quiet. We waited.

Finally, he spoke. "Wow, I'm not sure what to say. This is overwhelming. I wasn't expecting anything like this. I need some time to drink this in."

The road to mastery begins with self-awareness. Once you learn your traits and understand them, you will begin to see and feel them in action. One of the more difficult steps is to understand how your traits look and feel to others. If you think about the occasions when someone offered you specific and useful feedback about you as a person, you might have a hard time recalling anything that stands out. What Dave experienced is something we all crave, but seldom receive.

I don't hurry this part of the workshop. I can give people the opportunity to give their colleague the gift of genuine and specific feedback about how and why they are valued.

Your Headline and Signature Quote Provides a Compass to Mastery

To start the next conversation, I asked Dave, "If you had to pick just one strength as your go-to, which would it be?"

"Accomplishment."

As the first step in the exercise, I asked Dave to read through his trait report and underline sentences he felt captured his best strength. He did and then read those sentences to the group.

"Dave, why did you pick those sentences?"

"They really nailed me."

When I asked the team to boil their sentences into a short, memorable headline, Dave wrote for hsi, "I need to get things done." Then he shared a story with us.

"As a little kid, I can remember when I had a hard time leaving the sandbox to go inside before finishing my tunnel." One of Dave's colleagues chimed in with a *Larry the Cable Guy* accent, "git-r-done!" That became Dave's new headline.

"Okay, great job; now you'll have 10 minutes to search for a signature quote representing your strength."

Dave quoted Thomas Jefferson: "The harder I work, the luckier I get."

How To Judge a Virtue

What do you value or enjoy, simply for its own sake? I feel good and experience growth when I am honest, express love, engage in learning, show kindness, seek justice, etc. These are some of the virtues Seligman's team identifies. One simple test to determine what you value is to ask how it would feel if it were to decrease. Would I want less honesty? Less love? You get the point.

If you are curious about your character traits, you can take a free assessment to identify and rank 24 virtues.[28] Seligman also

---

28. "The 24 Character Strengths," VIA *Institute On Character*, www.viacharacter.org/character-strengths.

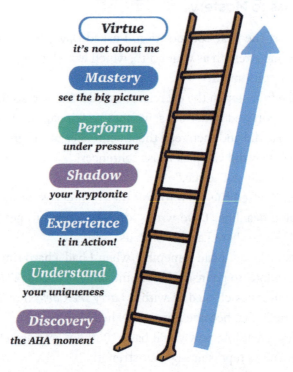

Finding Your Sweet Spot

Virtue
it's not about me

Mastery
see the big picture

Perform
under pressure

Shadow
your kryptonite

Experience
it in Action!

Understand
your uniqueness

Discovery
the AHA moment

uses the death bed test. "I wish I had spent more time (*fill in the blank*)."

Your Unique Purpose—Your Mission

Once you gain clarity about your genius potential, you are ready for a mission that demands your best to achieve it. A mission needs the following criteria:

- It daily activates your core strengths
- It demands your best
- It serves others
- It leads to virtuous ends

You may be surprised to learn that finding your mission is not searching for the Holy Grail. Fulfilling the four criteria is simple. Any number of paths can accomplish it, and your mission(s) will change over time.

The order is vital; establish a vision of your best self and then work on your mission to accomplish it. So why is there so much confusion about finding one's purpose? Why do I commonly hear, "I'm not happy; I think I need to do something different to find my why." Because "finding your why" has become such a common refrain in self-help books and among social media gurus, we think, "Yeah, of course. I need a why."

Simon Sinek's TED Talk and book *Start with Why* were revelations for me to better market my company. But, when someone goes down the "defining your why" path, I cringe because the book refers to companies, not people. I advise clients who worry about not having a personal "why" to relax. You don't need to reach far outside yourself for your 'why'. Maslow answered this question over 50 years ago. We are born with an innate understanding of our potential and a need to reach for that potential. That is the Genius Spark and why the starting point is to gain clarity on your potential best self.

Research to the Rescue

Two Stanford professors, Bill Burnett and Dave Evans, saw the same confusion and angst among students. Their research led to one of the most popular classes on campus, Designing Your Life. They have also published a related book, a workbook, and online classes open to the public.

In short, the book says first to define what you naturally do best and enjoy most. Does that sound familiar? They take you through a more elaborate process to clarify a vision of your best self, your ultimate purpose, and try to dislodge the notion that there is only one thing out there that will make you happy. The book provides examples of why there are multiple paths and not to get trapped by either/or thinking.

In one scenario, Michael, an engineering student, expressed that he was unhappy and ready to leave the profession and perhaps pursue a career in finance. Burnett and Evans asked him to keep a journal and write down the times he was most absorbed in his work and the times that drained him. Michael discovered he enjoyed most working on complex problems and felt drained working with challenging personalities. That is probably not a surprise, but Michael couldn't see the mismatch or connect the dots until he first determined what he loved doing and why.

He now loves what he does. Imagine if Michael never discovered his ultimate purpose and left behind his years of investment and all of his accumulated skills to pursue something entirely new—with no more certainty of finding happiness?

Your Ultimate Purpose—Process is Primary

"In any given moment, we have two choices: step forward into growth or step backward into safety." —Abraham Maslow

Most of my work, both personally and as a coach, focuses on the daily practices and habits of closing that gap between who were and who we want to be. Developing the mindset that the process is primary keeps our heads in the right space as we become our best selves—especially when the stakes are high.

Ben Crane earned his PGA Tour card in 2002. Just before he turned 30 in 2006, he was the highest-ranked American golfer under 30 in the Official World Golf Ranking. Injuries kept him sidelined for a few years, dropping him in the rankings. Still, he qualified for the PGA tour in 2009, which set up an incredible comeback story.

Ben struggled to find his old form and confidence. Pressure situations caused him to lose focus. He reached out to performance coach and Olympic gold medalist Lanny Bassham for help.

Lanny coached him to focus solely on execution, not outcomes. With Lanny, Ben focused on his stance, swing, and follow-through. He kept score on how well he executed the different aspects of his game.

In 2010 he qualified for the Farmers Insurance Open at Torrey Pines. Ben was one stroke ahead when he arrived at the 18th green in the final round. If he sunk a 30-foot putt, he'd win. At stake was $1 million. He sank the putt. His partner walked over to shake his hand, but Ben was confused until his wife ran onto the green and wrapped him in a big hug. "Did I win?" he asked.

What's Next: Putting Your Genius Into Action

Use Ben's example in your own life. Zero in on the process of self-discovery and consistent action. Meditate on your portrait every morning. Reflect on how you can close the gap between who you are and who you could be. Celebrate small wins. You will reach your highest potential through the compound effect of those small, daily steps.

Now let's get very practical. Here are seven ways to ignite your genius journey starting today:

1. Reread your Genius Portrait and strengths daily. This builds neurological pathways to tap into your potential.
2. Visualize using your strengths in new ways. Envision fresh applications at work and in your personal life.
3. Set micro goals based on your core strengths and current mission(s). Make them specific and trackable.
4. Experiment. Try small tweaks to add more of your strengths to your schedule.
5. Identify growth opportunities related to your top few kryptonite traits. Brainstorm incremental improvements.

DAILY PRACTICE

Reinforce *your genius paragraph*

Rehearse *visualize your day*

Reaction *from those around you*

Reflect *and then reimagine*

6. Share your portrait with others. Ask for input on how your genius shows up and how to express it more.
7. Join the Genius Spark community. Exchange ideas and find accountability partners. Don't go it alone!

You will unlock your full abilities over time by taking small but consistent actions. It takes an ongoing commitment, but the reward is a lifetime of fulfillment. Your genius journey doesn't have a finish line. It offers a never-ending path toward your best self.

Inventor Charles Kettering believed that "high achievement always takes place in the framework of high expectation." My expectation for you is high because your potential is infinite. I can't wait to see the genius you unveil. This is only the beginning. I hope the stories, insights, and practical tools shared throughout the book ignited your curiosity about your unique Genius Spark.

We started this journey by looking back at Rachel's story. She stared at the wall of childhood photos, wondering what happened to that curious, confident kid. Where did her natural motivations and talents get buried? Rachel represents many of us who have lost touch with our inner genius.

Yet Walt Disney reminded us that genius emerges when we embrace our originality. The research of George Land and Sir Ken Robinson proved that creative genius lives in all children. As Pablo Picasso said, the challenge is remaining an artist into adulthood.

The dilemma is that our education system, work, and social norms often train creativity out of us. We learn to fit in rather than stand out. But the good news is that it's never too late to reclaim your genius. This book aims to help you see your hidden potential. The psychometric assessments introduced can serve as a starting point to uncover your natural talents. However, the information alone is not enough. You must use it to paint a portrait of your best self—your Genius Portrait.

Let this portrait guide you in making small but consistent changes. Tap into your genius traits more often. Align your abilities with a sense of purpose. Develop the habits for continual growth. Fulfillment comes through engaging fully in the process, not just seeking the end result. Stay focused on progress, not perfection. See your Genius Portrait as a compass for your unique journey, not a rigid destination.

You now hold the map to navigate your own path. The stories and practical tools in this book have equipped you to reignite your inner spark and unlock your potential. But this is only the beginning! The work lies ahead in applying these lessons daily.

I challenge you to take the first step and craft your Genius Portrait. Let it guide you back to your core passions and abilities as a child. Recapture that creativity within yourself. Your genius has been waiting patiently for its moment to reemerge. Now is the time to unleash your full power and share your gifts with the world. Your brightest chapter is still unwritten.

One Final Story

When I was five, I imagined becoming an astronaut. My first grade teacher, Mrs. Stavoe, fed that dream. I made a scrapbook on the life of Enos, the space chimp. She wrote on a report card, "Rex has a wonderful imagination and loves to get up in front of the classroom and share his stories. I think he'll be a writer one day." I had forgotten about this until my mom passed away a few years ago, and my sister sent me her collection of just about everything in my life, including the receipt from paying the doctor's bill when I was born.

When I picked up that report card, I wept for quite a while. I realized that Mrs. Stavoe saw my Genius Spark and fed it. I missed it and buried it. I was never destined to be an astronaut. I gave that up early at our town's Frontier Days carnival when I got motion sick on one of the rides—I won't go into details. However, the spark she saw was my curiosity and drive to explore new frontiers and my love of stories. I cried because I wrote my first book at forty-seven and got my master's as a futurist in Strategic Foresight. I thought, "I made it, Mrs. Stavoe."

You and I are on the same journey. Some of us need a map or a guide, and some need our lives disrupted to wake us up so we can begin living our destiny. In my case, I had plenty of maps and guides, but I needed my life to face many challenges and fail many times before I'd quit playing it safe and start the journey of growth.

After the release of my first book, I found Mrs. Stavoe's address and sent her a signed copy. She wrote a cherished note back. She remembered back to 1960 how she encouraged me to follow this path. I hope somewhere along your journey, you can think of a Mrs. Stavoe, an unsung hero who saw and believed the best in you. If you can't, the good news is that it's not too late to rediscover and ignite your Genius Spark.

In the spirit of my first grade teacher, I hope this book has helped you identify what makes you unique, special, and rare.

Appendix 1

The Genius Spark Traits

What makes you, you? This section explores the unique personality traits that form the building blocks of who you are.

Over three dozen "Spark Traits" are identified here that cover a spectrum of natural inclinations, motivations, talents, and behaviors. Each trait falls into one of four zones:

Relating Traits: These interpersonal strengths help us connect.

Motivating Traits: These inspirational strengths galvanize us.

Thinking Traits: These introspective strengths drive insight.

Acting Traits: These exceptional strengths spark action.

The traits are presented alphabetically within their respective zones. Every description contains:

The Trait Name: A summary name for the trait.

The Zone: Whether it is a Relating, Motivating, Thinking, or Acting trait.

The Slogan: A short phrase evoking the core of the trait.

The Principle: The guiding maxim or essence of the trait.

The Description: A concise paragraph explaining the trait.

As you read each trait, consider whether it resonates with your natural motivations and inclinations. The traits most aligned with your inherent preferences are your potential "Superpowers" to embrace.

Let the exploration begin! Discovering your distinctive mix of Spark Traits is the first step in your journey toward self-understanding and empowerment.

Trait Summaries

Relating Traits: These interpersonal strengths help us connect.

Advocate – Relating – Welcome Host – EVERYBODY'S WELCOME

I champion those overlooked because I see everyone's inherent value. My accepting nature makes me an underdog's ally. I promote inclusion, believing diversity strengthens communities. My heart has room for all.

Authentic – Relating – Genuine Friend – GOLDEN RULE

I cultivate trust through transparency and unwavering loyalty. I can distinguish truth from falsehood and forge connections exclusively with those who reciprocate sincerity. Guided by the Golden Rule, my candor catalyzes nurturing enduring relationships.

Common Thread – Relating – Bridge-builder – WE ARE ALL CONNECTED

I recognize the universal bonds between all people. I build bridges of understanding between disparate groups. My inclusive worldview strengthens communities through empathy and celebrating shared humanity.

Diplomat - Relating - Peacemaker - FINDING COMMON GROUND

I discern misalignments within groups. My gift for finding common ground helps opposing sides understand one another. I navigate disagreements and strengthen team cohesion through empathy.

Emotional Awareness - Relating - I am attuned - TO STAND IN ANOTHER'S SHOES

I sense unspoken needs and emotions. My warmth helps people feel safe to express themselves openly. I can eloquently articulate feelings for those struggling to find the words. My care provides healing.

Fair - Relating - Life's Referee - IMPARTIAL AND PREDICTABLE

I avoid arbitrary choices, relying on impartial rules and standards. I hear all sides evenly. Calm objectivity and steadfast principles define my leadership. People trust my balanced guidance.

Good-Natured - Relating - Fun and Spontaneous - LET'S CELEBRATE

I naturally see the good, noble, and admirable qualities in others. I love to celebrate wins, great and small. I believe people try to do good things, and that goodness ultimately prevails.

Guide - Relating - Encourager - SUPPORTIVE FRIEND

I empower others to reach their potential by deeply understanding their unique needs and talents. My steadfast support provides the safety people need to grow. I walk beside them on journeys of self-discovery.

Loyal - Relating - Steadfast - YOU CAN COUNT ON ME

My relationships run deep because I give my all. I stand by people through rough times. They know I'll be there, rain or shine. My steadfast devotion provides security. I put others' needs first.

Mentor - Relating - Cultivating Potential - PLANTING ACORNS, CULTIVATING OAKS

I cultivate potential in people through supportive challenge and patience. My guidance helps them build capabilities and overcome growing pains. I spur development while providing a safe space to fail on the way to mastery.

Personalizer - Relating - Talent Scout - I'M DRAWN TO WHAT'S UNIQUE

I see people's uniqueness and where they fit. My chameleon nature adapts my approach to connect uniquely with each person. I help individuals recognize their rare talents and contributions.

Acting Traits: These exceptional strengths spark action.

Catalyst - Acting - Spark Plug - LIFE IS ACTION

I am an action-oriented trailblazer, igniting progress by fearlessly exploring new approaches. I thrive by learning through experience. Setbacks don't discourage me; they provide valuable insights to refine my path toward success. With my passion and determination, I transform stalled endeavors into an unstoppable momentum.

Confident - Acting - Assertive - RESILIENT AND RESOURCEFUL

My self-assurance comes from within. I know my abilities and limits. This conviction to overcome challenges expands my comfort zone. I let deeds, not words, define me. Resilience and willpower drive my success.

Drive - Acting - Git-R-Done - SENSE OF ACCOMPLISHMENT

I naturally set big goals and pursue them with relentless determination. Obstacles invigorate me. I stick to tasks with unyielding focus until successful completion. Milestones re-energize me to start the next endeavor. I feel restless without forward momentum.

Foresight - Acting - Master Planner - LIFE IS A CHESS GAME

I begin with the end in mind. Patterns reveal pathways around obstacles. I anticipate destinations before others. With the end in mind, I orchestrate intricacies efficiently on the journey to success.

Influencer - Acting - Daring - LEAVE A LEGACY

I live to make a difference and leave a valued legacy. I'm an independent thinker and look for opportunities where the outcome rests on my shoulders. I put everything I've got into every chance I get. Life is a hero's journey, and great work deserves recognition.

Integrity - Motivating - True North - DO THE RIGHT THING

My steady values guide my leadership. People trust my principles won't waver. I serve others and take courageous stands for what's right. My integrity compels me to align behaviors with beliefs. Purpose fuels my actions.

Reliable - Acting - Trustworthy - MY WORD IS MY BOND

My word is ironclad. I build trust by speaking honestly and matching my actions with my promises. People know I'll follow through with excellence. My commitment to truth keeps my reputation sterling.

Self-controlled - Acting - Diligence and Detail - BRINGING ORDER TO CHAOS

I operate reliably through preparation and self-discipline. Challenges become manageable when broken into executable steps. Structure and order optimize my productivity. I steadfastly follow through once I commit.

Single-minded - Acting - Pit Bull - HIT THE BULLSEYE

I tenaciously pursue goals with relentless discipline. Laser focus blocks distractions until I fulfill my objective. I plan meticulously and leave no detail to chance. My unwavering determination drives results.

Troubleshooter – Acting – Turn Around Artist – FROM BROKEN TO WHOLE

I derive satisfaction from restoring broken situations to wholeness. Turning problems into progress energizes me. I view crises with curiosity to discover creative fixes. My knack for healing drives growth.

Unshakable – Acting – Unflappable – NOTHING IS TO DIFFICULT

I hold an unflinching belief in myself that withstands turbulence. My poise conveys certitude to others, inspiring belief in their potential. My steadiness navigates change with determination. Doubt flees in my presence.

Vigilant – Acting – Light House – PERCHED ON THE WATCHTOWER

Perched on the watchtower, I stand as a vigilant lighthouse guiding others. My discerning eye detects subtle cues and brewing undercurrents. With composed clarity, I illuminate the wise path forward.

Motivating Traits: These inspirational strengths galvanize us.

Champion – Motivating – Will to Win – SCOREKEEPING IS KEY TO WINNING

I determine if victory is attainable and ignite the needed effort. Challenges strengthen my resolve. I set the thermostat to win. Losing motivates me to new heights. I channel pressure into determination until I optimize my potential.

Courageous – Motivating – Clear and Direct – COURAGE UNDER FIRE

My composed confidence and clarity motivate teams toward higher performance. I respect producers and truth-tellers. I don't shy away from healthy conflict if it leads to better outcomes. My courage helps me test limits and drive progress.

Fearless - Motivating - Now or Never - TAKE RISKS, FAIL FAST

I have a daring spirit that motivates others into immediate, bold action. I push boundaries, take calculated risks, and view setbacks as stepping stones. My adventurous example catalyzes teams to achieve more than they imagined.

Luminary - Motivating - Mastery - MOVE THE NEEDLE

I pursue mastery and preeminence in my work to meaningfully move the needle. My example motivates people to tap into their greatness. My dedication to excellence ignites progress. I want to inspire achievement that ripples through communities.

Optimist - Motivating - Can Do - THE UPSIDE OF LIFE

I spread infectious enthusiasm and lightheartedness. My upbeat outlook focuses on possibilities rather than problems. I celebrate small wins and believe in human goodness. Life is meant to be fun.

Paragon - Motivating - Best of the Best - IN SEARCH OF EXCELLENCE

I have an uncanny eye for excellence and potential. I take pride in perfecting everything I touch to sublime levels. My passion is helping dedicated people and projects ascend from great to magnificent.

Persuader - Motivating - Call to Action - TO ENGAGE AND INSPIRE

I craft messages that inspire action and light fires under complacency. My resonant words capture attention and ignite enthusiasm. My gift for persuasion propels change and mobilizes movement toward bold visions.

Thinking Traits: These introspective strengths drive insight.

Creative - Thinking - Outside the Box - IDEAS FUEL EVERYTHING

As an idea playground, my mind generates spontaneous novel connections. I fluidly blend perspectives into innovative solutions.

Unexpected moments trigger my imagination. My ingenuity manifests in offbeat humor.

Ever-Curious – Thinking – The Teacher – LEARNING IS A LIFE-LONG JOURNEY

As a lifelong learner, my curious spirit stays youthful and engaged. I retain information quickly, staying knowledgeable about trends. Teaching and sharing knowledge with others exhilarates me. The world is my school.

Objective – Thinking – The More You Know – SEARCH FOR TRUTH

I relentlessly seek facts and truth. My opinions and emotions don't outweigh the evidence in my decisions. I need proof points to believe. This skeptical approach leads me to make reasoned choices. My "why" and "how" questions unlock greater understanding.

Optimizer – Thinking – If–Then Analyzer – OPTIMIZE THE VARIABLES

I optimize outcomes by examining scenarios from all angles. Challenges are puzzles to solve uniquely. My contingencies prepare me to capitalize on circumstances. I enable others to achieve the best results through situationally adapted strategies.

Perspective – Thinking – Historian – IN THE BEGINNING UNTIL NOW

I honor the past, building on proven foundations rather than reinventing wheels. My decisions consider origins and precedents. I believe fortune comes from standing on the shoulders of giants. I tend to prefer time-tested approaches.

Philosopher – Thinking – The Oracle – STILLNESS ACHIEVES CLARITY

In stillness, my mind achieves clarity. Only after the shaken thoughts in my mental snow globe settle to the bottom can I see clearly. Virtual thought experiments allow me to examine concepts multi-dimensionally. I need quiet reflection for insights to crystallize.

Reservoir – Thinking – Subject Master – KNOWLEDGE STOREHOUSE

My sponge-like mind absorbs expansive knowledge across topics. Immersive learning provides an encyclopedic memory bank that informs my contributions. New mastery fills me with emotion and meaning.

Steadiness – Thinking – Process Engineer – PREDICTABLE AND RELIABLE

Habits and routines optimize my productivity. I value predictability and order. Consistent processes allow me to operate seamlessly, avoiding wasted energy.

Visionary – Thinking – What if? – BACK TO THE FUTURE

I see future possibilities and potential where others don't. Hope propels me past the constraints of the status quo. I orient more toward what could be rather than what is. My passion is to create a better world tomorrow.

Cautious – Thinking – Fail Safe – NO STONE LEFT UNTURNED

I anticipate obstacles, weigh risks versus rewards, and make careful choices. I'd rather be safe than sorry. My measured pace protects me from reckless mistakes. I listen and reflect before acting because foresight prevents problems.

Reflecting on Your Genius Spark Traits

Now that you have explored the spectrum of Spark Traits across the Relating, Motivating, Thinking, and Acting zones, it's time to reflect on which traits most align with your inherent nature.

Go through the traits again and select the twelve to fifteen that most resonate with you. These are likely your core superpowers.

To narrow further, choose your top five to seven traits that feel most effortless and energizing. These elite traits are your potential "signature strengths" to embrace and lead with.

Use the space below to record your top traits:

My Core Spark Traits (12-15):

_____

_____

_____

_____

My Signature Strengths (5-7):

_____

_____

_____

_____

_____

Looking at your signature strengths, consider the following:

- How do these traits explain your natural motivations and talents?
- How have these traits positively shaped your journey so far?
- How can focusing on these traits help you find purpose and fulfillment?
- How could leveraging these traits make you more impactful in service to others?

This exercise is just the beginning of a lifelong journey of self-discovery. Knowing your Genius Spark Traits lets you understand your unique genius and energy better. Embrace these superpowers within yourself, and unlock your potential to impact the world powerfully.

Appendix 2

Introducing the Genius Spark Ring System

Navigating the complexity of human personality can feel like trying to solve a Rubik's Cube blindfolded. With thirty-four talent themes, there are over 33 million possible combinations of an individual's top five strengths. The Genius Spark Ring system transforms this intricate puzzle into an intuitive deck of cards.

The story opens with Maria sitting down for her first coaching session. Her coach spreads a deck of cards; each color-coded into one of four suits. "Let's play a game of personality poker," he says. "These cards represent your natural talents categorized into four zones. Instead of memorizing every combination, we'll learn the languages of just four suits."

Maria draws five cards: two blues, one green, one orange, and one red. Her coach explains the zones:

Blue Ring—Relating Zone:

Interpersonal strengths for building relationships. Includes sensing, understanding, and connecting talents.

The Relating zone represents your ability to build meaningful connections with others. This comprises interpersonal talents like empathy, sensitivity, and understanding, allowing you to tune into people's feelings and perspectives. Individuals strong in the Relating zone are adept at building trust, resolving conflicts, and fostering relationships. They exude approachability and compassion. Colleagues may observe them listening and validating others' emotions during difficult conversations. They pick up on nonverbal cues and body language. Their warmth and care for people earn them trust and loyalty.

Green Ring—Thinking Zone:

Cognitive strengths for processing information. Contains input, analyzing, and deciding talents.

The Thinking zone encompasses your ability to analyze information and make reasoned decisions. This encompasses cognitive strengths such as pattern recognition, critical thinking, and judgment, enabling contemplation and strategy. Those strong in the Thinking zone delight in the life of the mind and feel energized by intellectual curiosity. They may be observed reading high-level books and articles during spare time or lost in thought while others chatter socially. They approach problems methodically, considering multiple angles before arriving at judicious conclusions. Their intellectual horsepower and objectivity make them invaluable advisors.

Orange Ring—Acting Zone:
Task-oriented strengths for taking action. Houses initiating, driving, and finishing talents.

The Acting zone represents your capacity to initiate action and drive results. This comprises task-oriented strengths like momentum, discipline, and resilience, enabling productivity and perseverance. Individuals dominant in the Acting zone operate in high gear and have trouble sitting still. They seize opportunities, tackle challenges hands-on, and persist through roadblocks. Colleagues may see them volunteering for tough assignments and putting in long hours. They maintain motivation and forward movement, providing momentum to propel teams. Their industriousness and determination deliver results.

Red Ring—Motivating Zone:
Inspirational strengths for energizing others. Comprises commanding, pushing, and energizing talents.

The Motivating zone encompasses your ability to inspire passion and activate commitment in others. This involves leadership talents like commanding presence, activism, and coaching that empower you to rally people to a common cause. Those strong in the Motivating zone naturally catalyze groups into action. They champion new initiatives and lead change. Peers often remark on their charisma and gravitas. Their bold vision and enthusiasm sweep others up. They build morale and commitment within teams. Their dynamism and conviction drive meaningful progress.

Maria's top strengths quickly come into focus: two in Relating, one in Thinking, one in Acting, and one in Motivating.

Her coach describes how she can understand herself and others through the intuition of a four-suit deck rather than the complexity of a Rubik's Cube.

The Genius Spark Ring System translates the intricacies of human personality into four color-coded zones, simplifying self-discovery and interaction by organizing strengths into Relating, Thinking, Acting, and Motivating suits. Let's explore the languages of these four rings.

The 15 archetypes in the Genius Spark system represent common combinations of strengths across the four rings. Understanding your archetype provides insight into your core motivations and patterns of thought and behavior.

The Archetypes

 The Connector: Strengths in all four rings make them great facilitators who can relate to anyone.

With dominant strengths across all four rings, Connectors have a gift for bridging divergent perspectives. Their empathy and sensitivity give them insight into others' emotions and worldviews. Their intellectual curiosity drives them to explore new concepts and ideas. Their enthusiasm and charisma draw people in and spark excitement. Their productivity and perseverance enable them to translate ideas into action. Connectors are agile chameleons who thrive on uniting people and spearheading change.

 The Servant Leader: Relating, Thinking, and Acting strengths make them great at building relationships and serving others.

Servant Leaders leverage self-awareness, intellect, and industriousness to serve others. Their listening skills and empathy build community. Their sound judgment steers growth and development. Their dedication empowers others to blossom. They lead through empowerment, not ego. Their quiet influence flows from service, not status.

 ### The First Responder: Strong Relating, Motivating, and Acting abilities make them adept at handling crises.

When crisis strikes, First Responders instinctively charge ahead. Their emotional intelligence and composure steer others through turmoil. Their inspirational presence builds resilience. Their swift decisiveness catalyzes order amid chaos. When able to take command, they shine brightest, empowering others to find the courage within. Their leadership ignites hope.

 ### The Juggernaut: Acting, Motivating, and Thinking strengths drive them to make bold changes.

Juggernauts generate momentum and change. Their bold vision and charisma rally others to action. Their intellect helps them analyze opportunities and calculate risks. Their drive and discipline convert ideas into reality. They are catalysts who spark action and transformation. Their dynamic presence leaves people feeling activated and inspired.

 ### The Energizer: Relating, Motivating, and Thinking make them great at inspiring others.

Energizers uplift and empower those around them. Their empathy, insight, and authenticity foster meaningful connections. Their analytical abilities help them identify others' needs and pathways to growth. Their inspirational presence fills people with self-belief and purpose. Their enthusiasm mobilizes individuals and teams to bring their best selves. Their warmth is infectious.

The Sage: Strong in Relating and Thinking, they provide wise counsel but prefer working behind the scenes.

Sages pair compassion and wisdom. Their warmth and emotional intelligence foster trust and openness. Their analytical abilities help them discern nuances and patterns. They distill these insights into judicious counsel. While modest and reflective, their guidance is invaluable. Leaders rely on Sages for perspective when navigating complexity.

The Pioneer: Thinking and Acting drive them to innovate and improve.

Pioneers have insatiable curiosity and a drive to experiment. Their intellectual horsepower hungers for new ideas and knowledge. Their diligence and perseverance enable them to operationalize theories into innovations. They relish diving deep into conceptual rabbit holes. While socially awkward at times, their original thinking and relentless tinkering lead to novel solutions. They flourish when given space to analyze and create.

The Project Manager: Strong in Relating and Acting, they excel at coordinating complex projects.

Project Managers adeptly steer multifaceted initiatives from conception to completion. Their emotional intelligence helps them navigate team dynamics and conflicting priorities. Their diligence and focus keep projects on track amid swirling chaos.

They translate broad vision into executable plans. While lacking big-picture strategic abilities, their practical orientation gets things done. Their superpower is delivering results.

The Innovator: Strong Thinking and Motivating zones create creative sparks for innovation.

Innovators combine analytical abilities with infectious enthusiasm to generate novel solutions and ideas. Their intellect tackles problems from new angles while their passion provides momentum. Colleagues may observe them bouncing between quiet concentration and animated brainstorming sessions.

The Catalyst: Strong Motivating and Acting zones generate passion and drive.

Catalysts are driven leaders who activate change through motivation and momentum. Their dynamism inspires teams while their determination drives execution. They may be seen rallying people around a vision while simultaneously rolling up their sleeves to get things done.

The Mentor: Relating and Motivating strengths make them great at inspiring individuals.

Mentors unlock potential in others through incisive listening, encouragement, and wisdom. Their warmth fosters trust and openness. Their motivational presence instills confidence. Their discernment senses unappreciated talents and barriers to growth. While lacking in technical expertise, they spur exceptional performance through insight and inspiration. Their gift is developing people holistically.

The Mastermind: All five top traits are Thinking, and these individuals have rich thought lives and deep insights.

Masterminds have tremendous analytical horsepower and thrive when applying their mental talents. They relish complex conceptual challenges and approach problems like shining light through a prism. You may find them studying academic papers, lost in thought or creative daydreaming, or analyzing situations from multiple angles.

The Warrior: All five strengths are in the Acting zone. Warriors live as perpetual motion machines.

Warriors are indefatigable forces of nature who power through obstacles with intense determination. They tackle tasks hands-on and lead by example. Colleagues may see them working long hours and volunteering for the most grueling but vital assignments.

The Guide: All five strengths are in the Relating zone. They have high emotional intelligence bordering on empathic.

Guides have exceptional emotional intelligence and thrive when connecting with people through insight and compassion. They build community by making others feel truly seen, heard, and valued. Their warmth and care earn trust and loyalty.

The Magician: All five strengths are in the Motivating zone, influencing those around them with inspiration and passion.

Magicians have a gift for inspiration that catalyzes groups to a higher purpose and performance. Their vision activates potential, while their encouragement builds confidence. They cultivate cultures where people feel energized and empowered.

Putting it Into Practice

The archetypes help simplify the complexity of personality and provide an intuitive framework for understanding motivations and behaviors. Identifying your archetype can provide powerful self-insight.

As we reflect on the unique contours of each zone, their interplay reveals our archetypal home. Consider when you feel most engaged and alive. Your primary zone likely aligns with peak energy states. Complement this with zones where you demonstrate natural skill, even if less energizing. Our secondary zones reveal what we do well versus what ignites us. By uncovering zone dominance and support, our archetype comes into focus. This clarity guides us in leveraging strengths while expanding capacities.

Exercise One:

1. List times you felt vibrantly energized and capable. Note the activities and talents you displayed in each instance.
2. Catalog what others compliment you on, even if it drains you. These reflect innate skills.
3. Identify your dominant zone(s) based on peak energy/engagement.
4. Pinpoint secondary zone(s) where you exhibit skill but less enthusiasm.
5. Use your zone dominance to map your archetype tentatively.
6. Read the full archetype description to understand your motivations and patterns further.

We unlock the code to access our best selves by illuminating our most active rings. This framework allows customized growth in the directions that catalyze us most.

Here is a potential second exercise to help someone identify and describe their one or two dominant rings:

Exercise 2: Pinpointing Your Rings

Now that you have a tentative archetype mapped based on your zones let's go deeper:

1. Re-read the descriptions for your dominant and secondary rings.
2. Highlight phrases that resonate with how you operate at your best.
3. Jot down examples of when you exhibited these strengths next to highlighted passages.
4. Extract two to four standout strengths from each ring to create an abbreviated custom profile.

For example:

Relating Ring:

- *Compassionate listener: Provide emotional support for grieving coworker*
- *Build trust easily: New hires open up about challenges*

5. Synthesize your standout traits from each zone into a personalized paragraph. Use your own language to capture your essence.

Sample:

My Relating skills shine through deep compassion and emotional intelligence, allowing me to tune into others' unspoken needs and provide heartfelt support. My Thinking strengths reveal themselves in my love of learning and applying new conceptual frameworks to solve complex problems.

6. Read your paragraph aloud or share it with someone close to you. Does it ring true?

By refining your zone strengths into your own words, you integrate this framework deeper to amplify your self-understanding.

Acknowledgments

This book and the Genius Spark system would not have been possible without the unwavering support, patience, and encouragement of my family.

To my beloved wife Lisa, who has been my companion on a shared journey of self-discovery to unlock our hidden potential and genius not just within ourselves but in our now adult children as well. Your enthusiasm in supporting others to find their inner brilliance has been invaluable.

To my children Michelle, Nathan, and Tyler who allowed their dad to grow through mistakes and have often gently but firmly reminded me of both my strengths and my areas for improvement. You three are a continual source of inspiration.

I am also profoundly grateful to the members of the Genius Spark Mastermind forum who participated in weekly calls over three years to rigorously refine the ideas, processes and tools behind the Genius Spark. Your insights and challenges throughout this endeavor have shaped this work immeasurably.

Sincere thanks to Meteor Education for their partnership in developing the initial software and to Trey Ryan whose talents brought an elegant web application to life. And deep appreciation to the publishing team at Meteor whose guidance empowered me to share these ideas through stories that have touched my life and work.

Finally, I'm thankful for the teams at Google and the International WELL Building Institute who generously served as pilots during an immensely challenging time. You expanded this vision and helped spark its full potential.

This book was a collaborative effort, and I am humbled by all those who lent their talents to make the Genius Spark system a reality. My hope is that it provides a catalyst for people worldwide to reignite their inner brilliance.

Author Bio

Rex Miller is a renowned expert in optimizing human and team performance, strategic foresight, and organizational transformation. With over two decades of experience as a consultant and coach, Rex has authored six Wiley books and received prestigious awards, including the CoreNet Global Innovator Award, the Industry Excellence Award, and IFMA's Distinguished Author Award.

Made in the USA
Monee, IL
09 March 2024

54208346R00108